THE POWER NETWORKING STRATEGY

The Personal Approach to Landing Your Dream Job

by Jay Arbetter

Copyright © 2017 by Jay Arbetter
All content is copyright 2017 by Jay Arbetter

All rights reserved worldwide.

No part of this book may be reproduced, redistributed, transmitted, retransmitted, translated, sold, given away, decompiled or otherwise circumvented by any means, electronic or mechanical, including photocopying, recording, or by any information storage or retrieval system, without written permission from the publisher, Manifest Publishing.

This book is designed to provide information and processes used by Jay Arbetter. Every effort has been made to make it as complete and accurate as possible, but no warranty is implied. Some names have been changed.

The information in this book is provided on an "as is" basis. Jay Arbetter and Manifest Publishing make no guarantees that you will experience the same results as the author. The author and Manifest Publishing also have no responsibility to any person or entity with respect to loss or damage arising from information contained in this book or from any programs or document that may accompany it.

Second Edition.

ISBN-10: 1-944913-13-0

ISBN-13: 978-1-944913-13-7

Ordering information:

Quantity Sales. Special discounts are available on quantity purchases by corporations, associations and others. For details contact Jay at Jarbet3539@aol.com

Individual Sales. Books can also be ordered directly from Amazon.com.

*This book is dedicated to
Jewish Family Service of Greater Dallas*

*They offer a continuum of care to children through centenarians who face challenges.
It was for their employment services division that I had the opportunity to begin my networking workshop seminars. I cannot thank their remarkable staff enough for allowing me to speak there while fine-tuning my seminar material.
It has grown to be a passion of mine and opened many additional speaking opportunities throughout the Dallas/Fort Worth Metroplex.*

www.JFSdallas.org

Contents

Preface iii
1 Take Charge of Your Attitude 1
2 Have Passion for What You Do 7
    Action Step #1: Discover Your Strongest Passions 14
3 Never Judge People 15
4 Pay Attention 21
5 Define Your Own Success 23
6 Value Your False Starts... 25
Jay's 31 Top Strategies for Landing Your Dream Job.............. 33
7 Find People with Similar Passions................................... 35
8 Connect with Your Advocates... 41
9 Create Lifelong Advocates 45
10 Build Your Network... 47
    Action Step #2: Create Your Worksheet....................... 49
11 Reach Out to People 51
12 Break Through Barriers to Your Success 57
    Action Step #3: Add a Column for Where You Met 64
13 Make All Your Follow-up Calls 67
    Action Step #4: Add in Call Back and Meeting Time 71
14 Prepare for a Successful Meeting................................. 73
15 Make the Connection 81
16 Keep It Professional 87
Success Stories 93
17 Reach Out to Special Interest Groups........................... 97
    Action Step #5: Special Interests Groups 102
18 Add Professional Associations and Advocates.............. 103
    Action Step #6: Professional Associations 107
19 Prepare Your Elevator Pitch... 109
20 Attend Career Support Groups 113
    Action Step #7: Career Support Groups 115
21 Remember Past Co-workers 117
22 Go Beyond Networking 119
23 What is Failure?.. 124
Epilogue 133

About the Author	137
Recommended Reading	139
Creating Your Excel Worksheet	141
Testimonials	145

Preface

Thank you for picking up this book. I hope these ideas help you as much as they have helped me and thousands of others. I want you to know that I did not write this book to help you get a job. I wrote this book so you can land your *dream* job. You know, that job you have always dreamed of having. That job that makes you excited to get up in the morning because you can hardly wait to get to work. I want you to have it all.

It has been said that 70 percent of the best jobs are landed through people who have recommended their peers for the position. People who are referred to a company by someone within the company, are the easiest people to trust and almost always get an interview.

Type "networking" into any browser and you will find at least 12 million results. (I found over 539,000,000 on Google!) That's a lot of information and opinions on what networking is and is not, and how to network effectively.

Regardless of whether you prefer to work online vs. getting out and meeting people, networking is still the most powerful way to land your dream job. Invest your time in taking the actions presented in this book, and you will find that networking is much more than handing out your business card. Networking is the lifeblood of successful people not only financially, but personally.

I will tell you right now, that I do not believe the 30-second elevator speech is relevant for landing your dream job. It might be good in the interview, but not so effective in networking.

What I'm going to teach you firsthand in the next few chapters is much simpler, and it relieves the pressure of you having to say the right thing. It makes people want to work with you to help you find your dream job. And, once you land your dream job, it will be a valuable asset to you and your new company in attracting high-quality new customers. This is a skill you will never want to be without.

You Are Always on Stage

Let me tell you something about myself. I struggled in my early years to be successful. I had many false starts and watched many around me achieve incredible financial success while I seemed to make one mistake after another. Then, I met Sarah.

Sarah went from being a stay-at-home mom with four kids to creating a business with over 30 employees. She was instrumental in teaching me how to network and get referrals when I was just a newbie in the financial services industry. When I asked her where she learned her business skills, she told me she had never taken a business class in her life. She was a theater major in college. She taught me that I'm always on stage and showed me that growing a business is about enthusiasm, passion, and making personal connections.

Master Networking

Because of Sarah and her mentoring and the teachings of a few others, I have grown my business to over $430 Million in assets under management in over 40 states and two countries. It works!

No matter what you are wanting to do in life, everyone will tell you, *it is not about what you know, it is about who you know.* Let's take it one step further. It is not only about who you know, it is about who you know that is out there and really speaking highly of you publicly. Who is your Advocate? Who is your fan, promoting you to others? Who is singing your praises?

The most successful people I know *intentionally* surround themselves with people who are willing to support them, provide mentorship and be an advocate on their behalf. The one question you should ask yourself right now is, *How valuable would it be for me to cultivate the kinds of relationships that have people excited to refer me to others?*

When you put into practice the strategies I share in this book, you will not only cultivate lifelong Advocates, your life will change forever for the better. You will find your life to be much easier, happier and more fulfilling.

Even though there are websites like LinkedIn, Monster.com and many other job boards, you will find that one-on-one networking is still the most powerful way to land your dream job. Always have an up-to-date resume ready, and make sure you have guidance on how to make your resume one that gets noticed.

Mastering networking will be that one skill which will elevate you and support you in anything you are wanting to do in life.

The most successful people I know surround themselves

with their Advocates, people who believe in them and will sing their praises.

Sharpen Your Axe

Once you learn how easy it is, you will want to create a prolific network of Advocates. But, before we jump into the how-to of creating your network, I am reminded of the story about two men who are chopping down trees right beside each other...

> *One older gentleman is steadily swinging his axe and has successfully chopped down two trees. Meanwhile, the younger man next to him is working up a mighty sweat and is swinging his axe like crazy; yet, he has barely chopped down one tree in the same amount of time.*
>
> *Seeing his sweat and frustration, the older man turns to his younger friend and suggests he takes a break to go sharpen his axe.*
>
> *The young friend replies, "I am too busy chopping down this tree to go sharpen my axe."*

How many times have you overlooked the obvious because you are frantically working hard with all the energy you can muster? Obviously, it takes less effort to chop down a tree with a sharpened axe, but these days we are living in such a frenetic society that we are 'so busy' and 'working so hard' that we forget to take time to go sharpen our axe before we start that big project.

Whether you are out of work and must find work quickly, or you have a job and want to find something better, I applaud you for taking the time to read this book. Sharpening your axe here can make the search for your dream job a lot easier. One good idea can save you a lot of time and energy in landing that dream job you've been searching to have.

Because I have a passion for people loving their work, it is my personal goal that everyone who reads this book gets at least one good idea that puts them on the path to landing their dream job.

So, let's get started learning the strategies to establishing an enthusiastic network of people who will be your Advocates and work for you on your behalf for years to come.

> GOOD LUCK!!!
> Jay Arbetter
> Dallas, Texas

1
Take Charge of Your Attitude

You cannot change your past, but you can change your attitude. Always remember you are on stage.

All of us will go through a difficult season at one time or another. We have good days and bad days. When I was a young financial advisor, I was taught by Sarah (my mentor and one of my best early clients) that the attitude you show to others everyday will make or break your future. At one time, Sarah found herself with little money and four kids to feed.

I found this quote by Pastor Charles Swindoll to illustrate what I learned from Sarah:

> *"The longer I live, the more I realize the impact of attitude on life. Attitude, to me, is more important than facts. It is more important than the past, than education, than money, than circumstances, than failures, than successes, than what other people think or say or do. It is more important than appearance, giftedness, or skill. It will make or break a company ... a church ... a home.*
>
> *The remarkable thing is we have a choice every day regarding the attitude we will embrace for that day.*

We cannot change the inevitable. The only thing we can do is play on the one string we have, and that is our attitude ... I am convinced that life is 10% what happens to me, and 90% how I react to it. And, so it is with you ... we are in charge of our attitudes."

Pastor Charles Swindoll

There are some building blocks that are prerequisites to unlock before you even can begin to think about meeting people and winning people over while networking. One is your attitude (which is one of the most important things in your life).

Like Pastor Charles Swindoll, I assert that your attitude in life will control how others see you and respond to you. In fact, the longer you live, the more you will learn that attitude is more important than the facts or the circumstances handed to you. It is more important than your success or your failure.

The beauty of it is, that every day we are given the ability to choose the attitude we want to embrace and exude. Remember, you cannot change your past, you can only change your attitude!

A Positive Attitude is Like Money in the Bank

Even when Sarah found herself at her lowest low, what she did have was a phenomenal way with people. She started and grew a business that had over 30 employees -- with no business degree. She had taken no courses in finance, economics or marketing. She credited most of her success to her education in theater. She was an actress by training.

Sarah taught me all about attitude. She told me, "When you leave your house, you are on stage. When you are meeting and working with people, you are on stage. Always remember this. You need to keep a positive attitude... always. No one wants to be with someone who has a bad attitude. It does not matter if you had a fight with your kids or your wife. It does not matter if you're going through a divorce or a civil lawsuit. No one wants to hear all that drama in a social setting or in a work environment. The more you express negativity, the more you will drive positive people away."

Remember your goal is to create Advocates who are crazy about you!

People love to be around positive people. The way you portray yourself attracts people of the same kind. This is a very important life secret. Like attracts like in friendships and in business. The more negativity you bring to life, the more negative people will want to be around you and the positive people will avoid you.

The more positive you are, the more positive people will want to be around you, and the negative people will slip away. If you have not noticed, wealthy people tend to have wealthy friends and angry people tend to have angry friends; the list goes on and on.

If you go on a date and spend the whole date talking about what a bad relationship you just had, I can promise you, the date will not go well. If you interview for a new job and you speak negatively about your last boss or the company you currently work for, you probably will not get the new job.

However, think how powerful it would be if you said in an interview how great your previous company was and how much you enjoyed working with your former co-workers. You would convey to your potential employer that you are sad that you were laid off, and you cannot wait to work for another great company as soon as possible!

Doesn't that feel completely different rather than complaining about your last company? Can you see how you would procure a better position with a better company with that positive attitude?

Learning to acquire and maintain a great attitude can impact many aspects of your life. This is not only about building a network so you can get a job; it is about you getting your dream job and doing something you are passionate about. It is about creating win-wins in every area of your life. It is about being happy.

See the Positive in Every Situation

When I was in college, I had a straight "A" average in every class except economics. I needed a high grade on the exam to even have a chance to get an A in the class. So, I did what many of us have done; I stayed up most of the night before studying for the exam the next morning.

When I arrived at class, there was the one thing no student wants to see after studying all night for an exam: a note written on the chalkboard in HUGE LETTERS explaining that the teacher was sick and the exam was postponed. If you are like me, you know that meant I would be up again one more night studying all over again. I crammed for the test and probably would not retain much of the information. I was very upset.

The next class was my accounting class. I slumped in my chair exhausted from staying up all night. Wouldn't you know it? The teacher gave a pop quiz that morning. What had I not done the night before? I had not read my accounting assignment. I bombed the quiz.

It clearly was not my day.

Then, I went to the food hall to get lunch, and just as life would have it, the student in front of me got the last hamburger patty. I was really looking forward to having a burger. Now, I knew for certain that my day was ruined.

However, what happened next was a life-changing ah-ha moment. For whatever reason, and I will never know why, the student behind me blurted out, "This is my lucky day!"

I turned around. I could not even begin to imagine what he was talking about. And, his next comment had a profound effect on the rest of my life. He blurted out, "I get a fresh, hot batch of hamburger patties! Yay!"

Now, I had never met him before. I had said nothing out loud, and I had no idea why he said that. But, what a life lesson it taught me! Here we were, both in the same position at the same time. I was upset over my morning, so I could only see the negativity in the current situation, and I was upset that I was going to have to wait for a burger.

He was in a very different mood and could only see a positive opportunity in the situation. In his mind, he was going to have a fresh, hot burger! I learned right then and there that it is your attitude that creates your perspective on things that are right in front of you. If you let your frustration control you, then everything you see will be seen in a negative perspective. When you are in a positive mood, everything will be seen in a positive light.

Never, ever let your past experiences cloud the vision of what opportunities might be right in front of you.

So, it is very true that a lot of life is not what happens to you, but how you react to it. The longer you possess a bad attitude in your daily life, the more you will alienate those terrific people around you, and the more likely you will miss a golden opportunity. So, Sarah was right. We are always on stage -- both for ourselves and for others.

2
Have Passion for What You Do

Stop settling for something just to get you by. Go for your dream job! Do something you are passionate about.

It is almost impossible to do anything effectively if you don't have a passion for it. And, networking without passion is nearly impossible, too. If you don't have passion, the people who you want to connect with will sense it immediately. You've heard that laughter is contagious, right? Well, so is apathy. If you are not excited about what you are doing, you will create apathy in your network and you are finished before you start.

Invest time doing things you love to do.

You will find your dream job doing what you are most passionate about. I will discuss how you communicate this later in the book. For right now, it is imperative that you not only know your passion, but that you can communicate what you are most passionate about to others as well.

I frequently give presentations to people at nonprofit organizations on *Networking the Old Fashioned Way* which teaches people how to land their dream job. I have met many people who have been laid off and hired somewhere else, only to find themselves laid off again after a six months or year. If you want a career or long-term employment, then you must have a passion for your work, for your company, and for your life. If you don't, you will hop from job to job feeling discontented, always wishing you were doing something else.

Passion and attitude are the building blocks to achieving success in anything.

Don't just go and get a job, go out and get your dream job. Have a passion for the company you go to work for. I am reminded of a guy working on the railroad tracks...

It is 100 degrees outside, and everyone is laying track. This man, Jack, is using the sledge hammer while his co-worker is holding the spikes that go into the ground securing the tracks. One afternoon, the president of the railroad comes barreling down the tracks in his private railway car to inspect the work. As the president gets out of the car, he sees this guy and yells, "Jack, is that you?"

At that moment, everyone is astounded.

No one can believe that Jack knows the president of the railroad. The president then invites Jack to come out of the heat and get in his car for chat. An hour later, they emerge and the president has his hand over Jack's shoulders. Each has a cold drink, and the president says how nice it was to catch up, and he looks forward to seeing each other again sometime soon.

When the president and his car leaves, everyone gathers around Jack. "How is it you know the president of the railroad?" they all ask.

Jack explains, "Thirty years ago, we were both standing in the same line looking for a job. We got picked to work together on the track, and we became good friends."

So, one man says, "I don't get it. How is it that you both started at the same time with the same job, and now he is president and you are still slamming away in the heat? What happened?"

Jack said, "It is simple, really. He went to work for the railroad, and I went to work for $5 dollars an hour."

The moral of this story is that if you are only there to work for a paycheck, then everyone will feel it. When you're passionate about your work, everyone will feel that, too. If you want success in your life, find your passion. Not only will you be more successful, you will be so much happier.

It doesn't matter if you are in sales or looking for your dream job, you want to connect with people who are as excited and passionate about your mission as you are.

When you want people to be your Advocates, you must convey just how passionate you are about your mission. Remember, you are on stage. That passion must be conveyed so that everyone you meet knows beyond a shadow of a doubt that you are in love with what you are doing or setting out to do.

Let me ask you. *Who is most likely to get laid off? The person who is passionate about their work and their company, or the person who comes to work every day just for the paycheck?* Of course, the person who is only there for the paycheck will get laid off first.

On the flipside, *who is most likely to get that promotion?* It usually will be the employee who everyone knows is passionate about their work and the company they are working for.

**Never be afraid to use the word 'passion' when you are talking about your work, especially when you are seeking your dream job.
It makes a great impression.**

When you are looking for your dream job, let people see how passionate you are about what it is you do, and how anxious you are to get back into the work force again. These are strong messages that make big impressions on people. Passion is highly regarded and very rare.

The most successful people I have met in life are passionate about their life's work. Without their passion, they never would have achieved their level of success. Life can be challenging and failures can come too often. If you are not passionate about what you are doing, you will tend to give up and move on before you can reach the level of success you are seeking.

Every athlete must face failure, losses, and injuries. If they lacked passion for their sport, they would quit. Passion is the fuel for the truly great people who have made a tremendous difference for all of us. Think of Thomas Edison, Steve Jobs, and Gandhi. They never gave up on their passion as they did not see themselves doing anything else in life.

The Wright brothers were told man couldn't fly. They didn't listen. They probably crashed a lot. If they had not possessed a passion for flying, they would not have developed that first plane. But, it did happen, and as a result, flying has become a worldwide standard of travel.

Most people who have become successful in business, including myself, have failed many times before they achieved success. We kept trying because we were passionate about what we wanted to achieve. Passion is the driver for your future. Without it, how will you keep going?

Find Your Passion

There are many books written on how to find your passion and purpose. I'm going to make this very simple for you. Go. Ask. Your. Friends.

During one of my *Networking the Old Fashioned Way* seminars, a dynamite lady stood up and said, "I do not know what my passion is. I have never had the luxury of following my passion. I have always had to work to put food on the table. Now I am in my late 40s, and I don't know what I want to do. How do I figure it out?"

I said, "Go ask your friends. Your friends know what you're passionate about. They know what you always talk about." Our friends know us. It is funny that when we are dating the wrong person, every one of our friends knows it but us.

The light went on for her and her face lit up!

She told me she didn't have to go ask her friends. She already knew what her friends would say (and have always said) about her passion. She told me that she is a perfectionist about cleanliness. When she goes in any hospital she is appalled at how sloppy and unkempt the floors are where patients are treated. She complained about it all the time to her friends.

I suggested she go to a hospital and take notes; write down every infraction she sees. As we all know, so many patients get sick in hospitals from all the infections they get while recovering. I suggested she take all those notes to an administrator and offer to audit the floors and bring back all her recommendations for a fee as an outside contractor.

She loved the idea, and said she had friends she could contact who would get her started. She was so excited about the idea, she could not wait to get out of my workshop and call them!

Do you see how energizing it is to have a dream job you are passionate about?

From my own experience, I came out of college with a degree in business, majoring in accounting. I found out quickly that accounting was not my thing. I had no idea what would be my path to success. I was young without any direction. Few of us really know what we want until we've tried a few things. I started my own businesses. Some were modestly successful, and others were dismal failures.

I had a college friend who for years begged me to come work with him. He was working in the investment industry, loved it and said it was right up my alley. It didn't sound fun to me, so I kept doing things my way. Nothing worked out.

Finally, I listened to him, and my life changed forever. Success was instant. I loved it, and everything came my way. If he had not insisted for years that I try this, I might never have. I never expected that this would be fun for me and something I would be so passionate about. But he knew me and kept after me until I literally was broke and had nothing else to do. So, the point is, if you don't know what your passion is, ask your friends.

Action Step #1:
Discover Your Strongest Passions

Go ask your friends what you are passionate about.
Jot down some of the things you like to do that you haven't made time to do. What do you really enjoy doing?

3
Never Judge People

People are not always as they seem. You never know who might be holding the key to your success.

You never know who can help you land that dream job. Making snap judgments about anything or anyone can cost you the missed opportunity of a lifetime. Here are a couple of judgements I made that have shaped my life considerably. One happened to me personally and the other professionally.

Looking for a Sea Ray

When I was in my early 20's, I was a water skiing instructor at my local YMCA, and I really enjoyed boating, however, I had never owned a boat. Later, but early in my career as a financial advisor, my wife and I decided boating and water skiing would be an activity our whole family could enjoy, so we set out to purchase a boat. Considering our two children were attending private school and my business was still in the building phase, we agreed buying a used boat would make the most sense for us.

We started looking all over for a boat, but we couldn't find one that met all our requirements. (After doing some extensive research, we decided we specifically wanted a Cobalt or Sea Ray.) We perused all the normal places like the boat dealers, Craigslist.com, and classifieds in our local newspapers. We had grown a little discouraged because the boats which were in good reliable shape were out of our price range. Eventually, summer ended, and we put a halt to our search until spring. We turned our attention to indoor projects as our new puppy had mauled several of our baseboards.

We contacted our favorite handyman, and what happened next, taught me a lesson I have never forgotten.

Someone Was Paying Attention

While our handyman was diligently working on the baseboards, my wife and I were discussing our disappointment and frustration concerning our boat search. Naturally, our handyman couldn't help overhearing our conversation, and he felt obligated to join in.

First, he asked if we had any specific type of boat in mind. We shared our wish list and what we really were looking for in a boat. To our surprise, he was the missing piece to our boat puzzle!

He had been painting a house just the week before for a client who mentioned he had a boat for sale. This homeowner told our handyman that his family wanted to sell their Sea Ray because their kids were now avid soccer players and as it was, their boat had only been used a half a dozen times. Now, it had sat in the garage for the last nine years.

This family wanted a good home for their once-loved boat, but they couldn't bear the thought of selling it to the boat dealer. So, they reached out to people they knew (like our handyman) and asked them to find them a buyer.

I credit that family with being savvy!

At that time, I never would have asked my handyman if he knew someone selling a boat (or anything else I was looking for). Who would think of that? I sure didn't. Well, the other family did.

They asked him to keep his eyes open and offered a nice commission if he found a buyer. And, just our luck, with the help of our handyman, we contacted that boat owner and discovered the boat of our dreams.

The Millionaire Next Door

Again, I was in the early stages in my career. I was really working hard to get business when I brushed aside a potential client because of my snap judgement based on how he looked and where he lived. I nearly cost myself one of my biggest accounts simply because I didn't take the time to ask the right questions

I had even read the bestselling book, *The Millionaire Next Door* by Thomas J. Stanley, Ph.D., which highlights that some of the wealthiest people live the most modest lives, while some of the people with biggest homes and fanciest cars barely have a dime to their name because they are living paycheck to paycheck. After 32 years of meeting and helping families with money, I know that this is the absolute truth, and if you haven't read the book, *The Millionaire Next Door,* I advise you to get a copy. You can easily find it for sale or at your local library.

One day, my Audi's entire electrical system quit. I could not power the windows or the sunroof. I went to the dealer, and they said it was a computer chip that had burned out and the chip was going to cost me $600. I was not going to pay $600 for a chip, because that was a lot of money for me. So, I started calling junk yards looking for a chip from a wrecked car. One junk yard I called, told me the largest junk yard in my area was in Waco, TX, a small town about an hour and a half away.

They told me, "If anyone has that chip, it will be them."

I called the next morning and sure enough, they had the chip; it was only $50.00. I kindly asked them to hold it, and I would pick it up. The lady said they don't hold parts for more than a day. On this day of all days it was raining cats and dogs. I really didn't want to get on the highway in that kind of weather. However, I had searched relentlessly, and this was the only chip I could find.

I asked her that if I purchased the chip from them, would it be possible for one of their people to install it for me. The nice woman on the phone said, "Of course, and at no additional charge."

In those days, I was not making anywhere near $600 a day, so I took off and went to this junk yard. When I arrived, I immediately noticed the massive amount of mud everywhere. I made my way to their office, and was greeted by a tall lady in overalls who asked, "How can I help you?"

I introduced myself as the guy who was here to pick up the chip and have it installed. She was surprised I drove all that way in the rainstorm, so she had not even made the request to have it pulled from the car. Immediately, she yelled in her microphone to a man named Charlie to pull that chip and bring it to the front office.

I waited over 20 minutes. Then this man who was bigger

than her and knee deep in mud boots, covered in tattoos, with grease all over his hands and arms, came in and delivered the chip. She told Charlie to take it to my car and install it. Thank goodness, this was only a three-minute deal. My car was under their carport, so I stood there with him and watched him install it. When he was done, my windows came to life, all for $50.00 plus the cost of gas to get there and back.

Then Charlie (who keep in mind was covered in tattoos, grease and mud) said he really liked my Audi and asked what I did for a living. I told him I was a stockbroker. (In the early 80s, we were not financial advisors, we were stockbrokers.) He asked me what that was, and I explained I help people buy stocks and bonds. To make it even simpler for him to understand, I threw in that I also worked with Certificates of Deposits (CDs) like the ones that banks offer.

Charlie asked if I would be willing to help him buy a CD. I was surprised he wanted me to do that, and I absolutely had no desire to open an account to help Charlie buy what I assumed would be a $500 or less Certificate of Deposit. In my arrogance, I told Charlie, "There are a lot of banks in Waco, Texas, and you can buy a CD from any one of them. I am sure any banker will be more than happy to help you."

Charlie turned to me and said, "I can't buy a CD in any of the banks in Waco."

"Why not?" I asked.

He said he was maxed out in all the banks in town as there were limits on how much the FDIC would guarantee in a bank. He needed a good broker to help him get all that cash that is uninsured out of the banks and into other investment accounts. (Hello? What an idiot I was! I had read the book and still didn't learn a thing!) I was stunned. I never saw that one coming. And, I never made the mistake of prejudging people again.

Had I not been just a little lucky, both of these really great opportunities early in my career would have passed me by! Remember, when you are looking for your dream job everyone is a potential gateway for introducing you to the person or company you are looking to work for. Do not prejudge!

4
Pay Attention

You never know when or how you might meet that person who can get you there.

I had been thinking about getting this book written and published for years. I asked a lot of people if they knew a good ghostwriter or editor who could help me make this book available so I could help more people find their dream job. I called the local universities asking for a top student in the English department who might be interested to no avail; the students didn't have the time to devote to it.

At every *Networking the Old Fashioned Way* seminar I gave, I asked if anyone knew someone who could help me. I would get some referrals, but I had not found anyone who I wanted to work with. I had met people who said they were good ghostwriters, but when I looked at their work, it wasn't what I was looking for.

I had all but given up when one day I was ordering a salad at the counter of a local café, and I overheard a conversation next to me. They were talking about the book that they were working on for another writer. I could not help myself from interrupting them because I wanted to learn more. It turned out that this person was a great writer and after talking, we agreed to meet again.

I was given a sample of her writing style, and it was exactly what I was looking for. You never know when or where you will meet the one person who can help you meet your goals. Things are never as they seem. Pay attention. Keep your eyes, ears, and heart open.

5
Define Your Own Success

Success is not measured by what you have; it is measured by what you want for yourself.

I often think of my client who was worth over $40 million because of his successful business (and, he was a young guy!) Because all his wealth was tied up in his business, I suggested it was time to sell. He had more than enough to take care of himself and his family for the rest of his life and theirs. I thought it was foolish to continue to risk everything for more, when he clearly did not need more.

His answer taught me a valuable lesson.

He said, "I can't live on $40 million. Do you know anyone who can live on such a small amount? With my vacation homes, club dues, and family trips, I would be broke in 10 years."

Around the same time, I also had a client who had $500,000 in his accounts. He often told me he never imagined having so much money! He had been a teacher his whole life, and he and his wife worked full time to provide for their kids. Most of the time, they had very little left over at the end of the month. But, they lived meagerly and saved what they could. When he was in his late 60s, he was astounded at how much he had. He honestly felt rich beyond his imagination. He and his wife experienced a wonderful and full retirement -- on *only* half a million.

PAGE FOR NOTES

6
Value Your False Starts

Most successful people do not start out successful. They've had a few bumps along the way.

I have been fortunate enough to manage investments for a lot of wonderful people who would consider themselves successful beyond what they ever could have imagined for themselves. But none of them, including me, started out that way. Like us, you probably have tried things that worked out okay, but not perfectly, or you have failed completely.

I can tell you my start out of college was anything but exceptional. In fact, by all measures, I was failing or only moderately successful at everything I did. I never let those failures or mediocre successes keep me from my dreams and goals. Finally, I found what it was that I should be doing, and then everything fell into place.

You will see that no matter where you are today, you can get to where you want to go or even go way beyond that. There is hope.

When I was 30 years old, I was ambitious and wanted to own a very successful business, but I had no idea how to define that for myself. What I did know was that whatever it was, I was not getting there.

When I graduated in accounting, I went to work for a public accounting firm. At first, I was put in the audit department. I hated that (and they hated me), so I was transferred into the tax department. That was an even worse disaster, and after only four months at the firm, I was fired. Not only was I fired, I was told to never apply anywhere else for any accounting job. It clearly was not my field. I call this a 'false start.'

If you are coming out of a false start yourself right now, I hope you are not beating yourself up. We kindly should allow ourselves to have false starts because we learn so much from them. First and foremost, we learn what we should *not* do. That is huge. The worst thing you can do in a false start is to keep pursuing the same things that clearly do not fit for you, as a way to 'fix' you. You do not need fixing. Learn quickly that there is something better for you, something you are better at, and move on.

In this false start, I found an opportunity to get where I wanted to go. I was passionate about owning my own business. All the accounting, economics and finance classes I took were to learn how to run a business. While I was doing taxes for clients at the accounting company that fired me, I happened to do a return for a commercial painter named, Tom.

Tom painted apartments when people moved out. He had no formal education beyond high school, but he was very street smart. Street smarts can take you a very long way.

When we were going over Tom's return, he asked me for some business advice; he had to figure out a problem. He was approached by the apartment managers to not only paint the apartments, but to also oversee the maid service and the steam cleaning. He really didn't want to do that, as he only knew painting. Yet, he was afraid to turn them down because he might lose the painting contracts. He asked me what he should do, and I told him to let me think about it. Shortly after that conversation, I was fired.

Here was the opportunity I had been waiting for -- to own my own business. When the light came on for me, I called him and suggested we form a partnership. I would run the maid crew, carpet cleaning services and bookkeeping, and he would do the painting and oversee all the painters we hired. If he could get an apartment painted in a day, I could get the maid crew in there and have the carpets cleaned the next day. Together, we would be able to turn an apartment in 24 to 48 hours. Think of the lost rent we could save the owners. Instead of waiting two to three weeks to get an apartment ready to rent, they could do that in one or two days using our services. We could command a lot for our service.

He loved it, and Apartment Troubleshooting was born. I was now going to be in business for myself! We offered our services to his current contracts, and they jumped on it. Fortunately, even though we had no money, we were able to secure bank loans with our contracts so we could hire maid crews and buy steam cleaners.

In one year, we had a very successful business and were limited only by the number of people we could hire and train. Do you see how this false start in accounting was the gateway to doing what I wanted to do? I do not believe in the connotation of 'failure.'

The only failure in any false start is to not find at least one thing positive to come out of it.

Keep Moving Forward

During my student driving lessons at age 15, my dad taught me that if you freeze in the middle of the intersection, you will get T-boned or run over. Once you start to make a decision, right or wrong, you have to do something. You must move forward.

False starts are like that, too. I am not saying to move hastily or make stupid decisions, but do not freeze and do nothing, either. I know people who are so afraid things might not turn out, that they never take any chances. In the end, they do not even come close to achieving their potential.

False starts hold many hidden codes to success.

As great as Apartment Troubleshooting was going, little did I know that I was in for another false start. Tom and I were growing like gangbusters, thinking we had the world by the tail when BOOM! The floor dropped out from under us with the 70's energy crisis created by the OPEC oil embargo. At that time, every apartment complex paid for all the utilities; there were no meters on individual apartments.

With utilities going through the roof, apartment complexes were hurting badly. The complexes could not raise the rents on the leases they had in place, so they were losing money and going into cash crunches; we were not getting paid.

We did not have enough cash on hand ourselves to

continue to pay our employees to do the work and not get paid for it from the complexes. Soon, we had to lay off everyone; just as fast as we had grown, we were out of business.

From this false start, I knew just how much I loved working for myself rather than working for someone else. I knew I wanted to be in charge of my own success, so I refused to apply for another salaried job.

I looked in the paper for any kind of business opportunity and found an advertisement from a hospital bed company that said:

"Top Commissions. Make as much money as you want to make. It is up to you, not us."

That is exactly what I wanted! I had never done sales, nor had I thought about sales, but I liked the sound of structure combined with being in charge of my own income. I went in and asked for the opportunity to learn to sell their product. There was a huge learning curve. After a few weeks, the sales trainer told me that sales was not for me. He recommended to the senior partner that I not be hired.

The senior partner saw something in me and asked if I wanted to be trained to sell or not. I wanted the freedom and the money, so learning something new made total sense to me. I was game. The senior partner took me under his wing and taught me how to set up the sale and close the sale.

By the end of three months, I was their #1 salesperson.

Once again, I was on my way. (Of course, I didn't know it was going to be another false start. You do not see false starts coming. You only see them after they happen.) Being the #1 salesperson with a business degree made me more valuable to the company than I really wanted to be. Who knew *that* could be a problem?

The company expanded to a new office in a different town, and I was chosen to open it. I had no interest in working for anyone in any kind of management capacity. I loved being in charge of my own time and making the money I wanted to make. But, they said that if I didn't take the job, they would have to let me go as they only wanted trained sales people who would move up the ladder when they asked. I was forced into becoming a manager. I lost my freedom, and I hated it.

I had to move, hire other sales people (train them), hire office staff (train them), and send reports into home office. If that wasn't bad enough, right after I got it fully up and running, the company was sold and the new company put their own managers in place.

Then, I was told if I wanted to stay, I would have to move to another state and take a position higher up in management. That would take me completely out of sales and move me into a totally salaried position. I flat out said, "No."

Here I was, unemployed again, another false start. But, what a skill I learned! I learned how to be a crackerjack salesman, something I never knew I could learn, much less, do it at such a phenomenal level.

Here Is Where Everything Changed

Remember, earlier in this book, I said to that lady that her friends knew what her passion was? Well, my college friend was in investments and doing very well. He was making more money than I ever had made, (and, I had made some good money). Finally, I was willing to listen to him.

George told me I was born to do investments. Investments would allow me to use all my business education, and with my sales skills, I could really do well bringing in new accounts. He said I should move to his hometown and go into partnership with him. I could bring in the accounts, and he would invest the money until I learned how.

I said, "Done!"

I moved to his hometown and got my commodity licenses to be legally able to sell. Initially, I did not completely understand everything I was selling, but I was good at it. George did the investing and within months we were one of the top teams in the city for opening new accounts. Then, the manager came to me and asked me to take over the sales manager role. This time, I could see the trap coming. I refused the job.

Of course, the manager was very upset, but agreed to not bother me about it if I agreed to lead classes in the office. I taught the classes without pay. I didn't want to work for anyone for money. Shortly after, an opportunity arose for me to move back home and work as a broker for the same company. I accepted it, and George and I split up.

At some point, I realized I didn't love being a commodity broker, and I decided to sell my clientele to another broker. Once again, I found myself without a job. This was my last false start and the one that put me squarely on my path to success beyond my wildest imagination.

What I learned was I love investments and sales. This was what I wanted to do the rest of my life. I just needed a really big company behind me.

Getting Closer to My Dream Job

In 1985, I had a friend at Merrill Lynch whom I had met at a conference. He set me up with an interview, and I got hired immediately. I have never looked back.

When Merrill Lynch failed in 2008 and was bought out by Bank of America, it was not an issue for me. I had my own team, my own clients, and I was in control of my career -- for the first time in my life. When we made the decision to leave Bank of America, it was no problem and our clients went with us.

So, let's look at what it takes to build a business from scratch. The networking skills that I learned to build my business, will be the same skills that you can use to land your dream job or career.

Jay's 31 Top Strategies for Landing Your Dream Job

1. Take charge of your attitude.
2. See the positive in every situation.
3. Have passion for what you do.
4. Invest time doing things you love to do.
5. Passion and attitude are essential to success in everything.
6. Never judge people. You never know who might be holding the key to your success.
7. Pay attention. You never know when you might meet the person who can help you.
8. Define your own success.
9. Value your false starts.
10. Unite with people who have the same interests and passions as you do.
11. Track your network to build your network of Advocates.
12. Networking is not about you. Focus on the other person and tell them what you like about them.
13. Do not meet with people you do not like.
14. Some people help, while others simply do not help others. Focus on the ones who help.
15. Know when to use the 30-second Elevator pitch and when to avoid it.
16. Getting people to be lifelong Advocates of yours is a skillset we develop. Keep practicing!
17. Networking is not to 'get a job' – it helps you find your passion, connect with people you know, sharpen your tools and land your

dream job.
18. Passion is infectious.
19. Being negative is ALWAYS a deal killer. Make lemonade, always.
20. You are always on stage, bring your best, be positive, and be passionate.
21. Networking is a verb: cultivate people who can be your Advocates. It makes everything easier.
22. Dress professionally.
23. Avoid isolation. Get out there and meet people!
24. Do not let a past bad experience cloud your current experience.
25. If you interrupt a group of people talking and they turn their head only to respond, that signals they're engaged in a closed conversation, so move on. If they rearrange themselves in a more open posture they are open to include you, step in and take advantage.
26. "Bother your friends!" – if your dream job was locked in a vault with $50 Million, you would not hesitate to ASK EVERYBODY you know, *who has the key?!*
27. Stay in control of follow up. Never hand out a card or resume in a social setting.
28. Never miss a follow up appointment.
29. Always send a thank you note. Always. Always. Always. This is a Cardinal Rule.
30. False starts are hidden codes to success.
31. People will only be an advocate for you when they know how much you like them.

7
Find People with Similar Passions

When someone has the same passions and beliefs you have, it is amazing the length that they will go to help you succeed.

Now that we have introduced some of the building blocks of successful networking, let's look at what networking really is: Networking is a socio-economic business activity by which business people and entrepreneurs meet to form business relationships and to recognize, create, or act upon business opportunities, share information and seek potential partners for ventures.

Networking is both a noun and a verb.

Networking as a Noun

It is a supportive system of sharing information and services among individuals and groups who have a common interest.

Networking as a Verb

It is cultivating people who can be helpful to one professionally, especially in finding employment or moving to a higher position. Or growing your clientele or business.

The keywords in the noun are *common interest*. People are much more likely to want to be your Advocate when you share a common interest. When you both share something in common, be it a love of music or the arts or building homes for the homeless, then you're more likely to get their genuine support.

Someone who is a total stranger or referred to you, who has nothing in common with you might be a great Advocate, but that would be rare.

If you love art, go to art exhibits, everyone you meet there will easily see how passionate you are about art because they will be passionate about art, too. Maybe you like to shoot guns. Well, then go to the gun range. Everyone you meet who likes to talk about guns will know you're passionate, too. So, why would your personal life be any different? People love to be around people who are excited about what they do, all day, every day. It doesn't matter if you are working with clients, fellow employees, or managers.

Advocates Share the Same Passion

One of my greatest passions is road bike riding. I typically ride 36 miles on Wednesday mornings and 50 miles on Saturday mornings. Around 2008, a friend of mine asked me to join his team to ride the MS 150, a 150-mile bike ride to raise money for Multiple Sclerosis. The first day was 85 miles and the second day finished the ride with only 65 miles. In all my years of biking, I had never ridden 85 miles in one day, but I thought, *Hey, how hard can it be if you're in good shape, right?* So, I decided to do it.

I registered and received a package with an MS shirt and a number to attach to the shirt. My friend had a whole team ready to go and told me where they would be meeting at the start of the race.

I took the package apart and read all the details about the starting time and the location of the start. I took out my number and set it on my dresser. I left the shirt in the package to be ready the morning of the race. It started at 7:00 a.m. I wanted to get there by 6:15. I woke up ready to go, but could not find the package with my shirt. It wasn't there!

Not wanting to wake up my wife by rummaging around the bedroom in the dark, I grabbed another bike shirt out of my drawer, attached the number to it, and off I went. When I got there, I found 3,000 riders and no team. I was on my own.

The gun went off, and I was on my way. The first 50 miles was a breeze. I ate lunch, took a nice rest and started for what I expected to be an easy 35-mile stretch. Nothing could have been further from the truth. The next 35 miles were mostly up and down hills. The wind picked up making it even harder. To make matters worse, the sun came out, and it was close to 100 degrees. I think it was one of the warmest May days in Dallas history. Regardless of all of this, I kept going.

There was a rest area every 10 miles or so. I made the first rest area feeling okay. But honestly, it was one of the hardest 10 miles I can remember biking. So many riders had given up. They lined the road waiting for the van to pick them up; the heat and the wind and the hills were just too much.

After cooling down and taking lots of fluids, I decided to try to make the next 10 miles to the next rest area. I swear they moved it. I was so hot and I was so tired, I couldn't find it. Finally, I had to pull off the road under a tree with other bikers to cool down and drink more fluids.

Again, I started on my way. I found the rest stop and rested again. I only had 15 miles to go. The going got harder and the harder it got, the more bikers there were giving up. I found myself stopping about every three miles now to cool down and get fluids. That didn't really work as my legs started cramping. I know from my extensive biking experience that once you start cramping up, you are done for the ride.

I didn't want to quit, but I felt it was coming. I got off my bike and really stretched, drank my recovery powder, ate lots of calories and took some time. The cramps went away, and I decided to start again. (As you can see, I do not quit easily.)

I do not know how far I got after that, but my GPS tracker said I was at mile 80. I had just finished a hill and nothing was left in me. I was finished; to proceed would have been risking my health, and I was not going to do that. I pulled my bike over and sat in the shade, waiting for the van. A few seconds later a police officer pulled up and asked, "Are you okay?"

I said, "Yes, but I am spent. Totally spent." There absolutely was nothing left in my tank.

He said, "You're at mile 80. There are only five miles left to the finish line."

I replied, "Sir, if the finish line was across the street, I could not get there. I am done."

He said, "OK, but the van is so busy picking up riders, you could be here another 45 minutes."

I said, "I have plenty of water. I'll wait."

A few minutes later, a biker came by asking if I was okay, and just as I had told the officer, I told him I was done, totally spent, could not go another mile. He said, "You know the finish line is only five more miles." I shook my head that I knew that, so he went on riding.

Then this guy who looked big enough to be a linebacker for any team in the NFL stopped and said, "You okay?"

I said, "Yes, I'm good."

He questioned, "You aren't quitting here, are you?"

I replied, "Yes. I can't move. I am totally spent."

He encouraged me, "No you're not. This is the last hill and then it is flat and turns so you're not into the wind. I will ride the hill with you and block the wind for you, and you can draft me. And, no matter how slow we need to go, you are going to finish."

Again, I questioned, "Really?? The last hill?"

He said, "Yes, I rode this last year."

I said, "Well, if you're going to block that wind and go slow, maybe I can get over this last hill." At that time, I averaged about 16 to 17 miles per hour on my weekly rides. I had an average this day of about 13 miles per hour. So off we went. I took that hill at no more than four miles per hour. We got over that hill, and true to his word, he totally blocked that wind for me. If I was left to battle that wind and the hill and the heat on my own, I never could have made it.

Once we turned out of the wind and started riding on flat and downhill terrain, I got my strength back. We started talking as I rode next to him. I asked him his name, and he told me his name was Fred. I thanked him so much for taking the time to get me to the finish line. He said, "I didn't do it for you. I did it for your shirt."

I had no idea what he was talking about. So, I asked, "What do you mean 'my shirt'?"

He said, "You're wearing a Susan G. Komen cancer shirt. My wife is a cancer survivor. And, anyone who supports cancer is not going to stop five miles before the finish line if I have anything to do with it."

Wow!!!!

If I had worn the MS 150 shirt, I never would have finished the ride that day. I picked that shirt out of my drawer in the dark. And only because of the Komen shirt did he stop to make sure I finished. What a powerful lesson that was in life.

When someone has the same passions and beliefs you have, it is amazing the length that they will go to help you succeed.

8
Connect with Your Advocates

So, what is the process for starting to build your network? Connect with people who share the same passions that you have.

First, I highly recommend that you make the time to read a book called, *Never Eat Alone* by Keith Ferrazzi and Tahl Raz. It is a must read. When I started my career as a financial advisor, it was 1985, and I didn't know anyone.

Times were different then, it was a cold-calling environment. You may or may not remember that cold calling was much easier as there were no cell phones and no Caller ID on every phone. Cold calling was the way to get connected with new people. I bought a telephone list of 3,000 names of people 55 and older because they generally had all the money and no expenses. This group of people on my list lived within three miles of my office. I started calling.

My goal was to call 100 people every day with the intention to talk to 10 people and get at least one appointment. If I could get 10 appointments over a 10-day period, I usually could close one of them and have a new account.

As it turned out, I was terrible cold caller.

In fact, the success rate for new financial advisors doing this kind of prospecting was 10 percent or less. I had to find another way. I opened a few accounts and met some people socially. This is when I met Sarah who was far more valuable than the commissions I received on her investment account.

Sarah taught me the hidden codes of building a successful business through networking. She encouraged me to find people who had the same passions, interests or hobbies as I did. I have taken the building blocks she taught me and built a clientele that stretches over much of the United States and in two countries.

To find those people who have your same passions, you must know your own passions first! I know that I already had you start your list on page 14. Continue to add to your list. Add your hobbies, too.

This is important for a lot of reasons; you not only need to know them, but you must be able to articulate them in a job interview or a networking opportunity. How can you land your dream job if you do not know what it is you really want to do or cannot articulate it clearly? That's right, you can't.

For the record, I am totally against an elevator speech. I find them boring, and so does everyone else. Most people automatically will tune out. Let's use this example: If you're at an art exhibit because you really enjoy art, and you meet someone for the first time, they very likely will ask you what you do.

If you've practiced your elevator speech, you will say something like, *Right now, I'm looking for a job doing XYZ* followed by your redundant elevator speech. And, you are done before you even know it. The likelihood of that person caring is zilch. You've given that person nothing of any importance to really care about.

A much better response is, "I am currently looking for a job. I would love to take you out for a cup of coffee, find out more about you and let you know the kind of work I am passionate about. Perhaps you might know someone who works at one or two of the companies where I'd really love to work. Do you mind giving me a few minutes of your time? I would greatly appreciate it."

When you are both passionate about art and have had an enjoyable conversation, they generally will respond with something like, *Sure, any time! Why don't you give me your contact information (or your business card or resume,) and I will get with you.*

Never hand out a card or resume in a social setting.

Once you give someone your business card or resume, you are no longer in charge of the follow-up. It is always better to say something like, *You know what? I don't have one on me right now. If you have a card or if I can get your number in my cell, I will send you all my contact info right away.*

This leaves you 100% in charge of the follow-up. I learned this when I was in training to be a successful financial advisor. My instructor told me to never hand out a card, and I have never handed out a card in a social setting my entire career. I always get theirs so I can follow up with them.

As my career got going, our firm had professional coaches train us in how to build a huge business. I learned so much from them. Whether you are building your network to find your dream job or building your own successful business, it all works the same.

I also was trained to *never have clients you do not like talking to* and *do not spend time networking with people you do not like*. Period. It will never work out. The authentic connection just is not there, and they will never be your Advocate. Invest your time and energy in people who you feel connected with and enjoy being around.

9
Create Lifelong Advocates

People will only be an Advocate for you when they know how much you like them.

That same instructor who told me to only be around people who I like, also told me to go back and look at everyone in my network (including all my clients), and get rid of the people who I do not like. He told me to get rid of any of the ones who I do not enjoy.

Even my clients? I thought. Wow. I didn't want to let go of that income, but he was right. Life is too short. And people you do not like can ruin your day and your attitude for the ones who you do like. If you do not have the right attitude, the ones you do like will not want to be around you, then you will be stuck with the ones you do not like, so just let them go now.

So that day, I culled my entire network and clientele to include only my favorite people. Of course, everything got more fun from that point on, and it has never stopped. I truly love the clients I have and the people I hang out with.

The Game Changer

Then another coach came in, and he really put the icing on the cake for me. His philosophy was this: No one will be your client or consistently be your Advocate just because they like you.

What?

He went on to say that people will only go to bat for you and/or become your lifelong clients when they know *and feel* how much you like them. If they do not feel that, you are in a losing battle.

It is so important that you let people know that you admire them and like them. (This takes more practice for shy people, but it's a game changer, so you will want to start doing it right away.)

That day, I started calling my clients to tell them what I appreciated about them. (I already had pared down the ones who I didn't enjoy working for, so it was natural to let my clients know what I admired about them, and how much I loved working with them.)

You would not believe the response I got. I was shocked! They said, "Really? You feel that way about me? I had no idea."

I said, "Absolutely, I am only sorry I haven't said it before. I love working with you. You are such a great person."

That was the end of my cold-calling. I haven't made another cold call since. I haven't had to. The referrals started coming in like crazy, and they have not stopped!

So, now that you know the importance of making people your Advocates and how easy it is, let's start learning how to build your network.

10
Build Your Network

What we focus on expands. If you want to build your network into a prolific group of Advocates, it is time to start organizing your networks.

You may or may not know, you already have a network. However, because you are reading this book, you probably haven't consciously kept track of who is in your network, or put much attention and focus on growing your network.

What we focus on expands.

There are many ways to start building your network. And there are just as many ways to keep track of your network. We have so much technology at our fingertips (literally) that it is crazy not to use it. To start tracking your network, find an app for your phone, an online computer program, or go old school with a notebook and pencil; whatever works best for you is what you do.

What I'm going to share with you is my super simple system using an online worksheet like Microsoft Excel, Google Sheets or Apple Numbers. And, by no means should you limit yourself to my method.

> **To make this as easy as possible for you, I have created a Microsoft Excel worksheet for you to download. You can go to:**
>
> www.ThePowerNetworkingStrategy.com
>
> **It is a Facebook group page where you also can get support from others looking for their dream job. (This is only if you are interested. There is no obligation whatsoever.)**

Start by thinking of EVERYONE you know. Think about your family, your friends, any past co-workers, your connections at your place of worship, people you know through activities and hobbies, your hairdresser, your handyman, anyone else you can think of who you have known through the years. This will take time, as you will not think of everyone right away.

Next, go through your phone contacts to come up with more names. Go through your email list. If you have Facebook, make sure you look at all the friends you have there. Do the same for LinkedIn, Twitter, Instagram, etc. Check all the people who have asked you to connect with them.

Get your list as long as possible.

Action Step #2:
Download or Create Your Worksheet and Start Adding Names

1. Download the Microsoft Excel worksheet or create a worksheet for yourself on paper, with an app, or computer program that will work for you.

2. Name the sheet PERSONAL. You will most likely want to create multiple worksheets with different sections for different groups of Advocates.

3. In Column A, start to list all the people you know using one row per name

4. In Column B, add their phone number and/or email address

5. In Column C write down what you have in common with them. See example on the following page

6. Remember anyone you have previously worked with. This is very important.

The Power Networking Strategy

Personal Connections

Advocate	Phone Number	Common Interest
John Doe	123-456-7890	chess
Betty White	234-567-8901	fishing
Susan Clark	345-678-9012	IT
Lori Frank	456-789-0123	We both have kids.
Julia Moon	567-890-1234	investments
Sam Smith	678-901-2345	guido's pizza
Ali McGregor	789-012-3456	LinkedIn
...	...	...

11
Reach Out to People

It is not about you. It is about the other person.

When you are looking for a job, you initially will need to reach out to everyone you know. That is why I had you create such an extensive list.

Now, let's look at Column C on your worksheet. In this column, you wrote down what you have in common with each person. This is very important as you will not always remember where you met someone or what you have in common with them. You need this because when you sit down with someone to ask for help, the first part of the conversation will be about what you have in common.

The key part about using this information is that it does a couple of things for you: First, it immediately takes the conversation away from you. Nothing about networking is about you. It is always about the other person. (This will also help you get over the potentially horrible feeling of being rejected if they do not really show much interest in helping you.) And, it is not that horrible. It is not personal. Remember, it is not about you.

There are lots of jobs that are never posted anywhere. Typically, if a company has an opening, the management asks everyone in their company if they know anyone who might be qualified to fill the position. Often, management would prefer a current employee recommend someone who they know, rather than post the job and deal with the process of looking at resumes of complete strangers.

If the job is filled this way (and many are), the jobs never get posted. So, if you do not have your network out there working for you, you probably would not even know of the opening for your perfect dream job.

I have no idea how many great jobs are filled this way, but I can tell you from personal experience that I have helped many people get jobs in my market area – jobs that never were posted, because I filled them.

Many people from my workshops have reached out to me to help them connect with others and find their next job. It is a passion of mine to help those out of work to get back into the workforce as soon as possible so they can be doing something they love.

Ask for Help

When I start my workshops, I always ask, "What are the reasons that will keep you from asking your friends or family for help to find your dream job?" I get lots of answers. I'm going to share them because maybe you feel the exact same way about some or all of the answers that I hear from participants:

1. I am not worthy of anyone wanting to help me.
2. I don't want to feel obligated to anyone who might help me.
3. I don't want to impose on my friends or others.
4. I don't like rejection. They might say no.
5. I don't want to waste my time as no one will help me

anyway.
6. I don't want to waste their time.
7. It will feel awkward and uncomfortable if I ask.
8. I don't want them to know I've lost my job.
9. I don't want to risk someone hitting on me if I ask for an opportunity.

Regardless of any concerns you have about asking for help from others, you need to build that network of Advocates that will help you find your dream job. You will want to perfect your skills and learn the personal approach to power networking. Let's go back to the worksheet. It might be hard for you to call the people on your list, but look at it this way...

What if I told you there was a vault with $50 million dollars, and one of the people on your list has the key?

As you read through the list of objections, you might have found yourself saying, *Yes, that is me for sure.* Or you might have come up with a reason or two I have not heard of yet. Look at the list and the other reasons you may have that would prevent you from asking for help.

Now ask yourself, *Which one of these reasons would keep me from asking anyone I know if they have the key to the locker with $50 million dollars in it?* Would fear of rejection or being told no, keep you from asking? Would the feeling of possibly wasting your time or theirs, keep you from asking? I do not think these reasons or any others would keep you from asking. In fact, I doubt you can think of one thing that would keep you from asking someone you know if they have the key to the $50 million dollars.

Put away any barriers you have asking for help, and let's get your network working for you. You are now on your way to being in control of your future!

Here Is the Secret

Just as there is that one person who holds the imaginary key to the $50 million dollars, there is that one person on your worksheet who holds that key to your dream job. And, when you do this right and reach out to them letting them know what you admire about them and why you like them, they will not only help you find your dream job, they also will be a resource to you for the rest of your life for anything you want.

Now, don't get complacent with your worksheet as it is dynamic, meaning it will always be changing. You will add people in Column A as you meet them, and take people off your worksheet if you clearly see they are never going to be a resource for you. Maintaining and focusing on a strong, well-documented network will change your life in ways neither you nor I can imagine sitting here today.

If you **don't** think it will, just look at any new mother. Young mothers are the best and most natural networkers in the world. They help each other every day. They meet in **playgroups, in schools, and in small social settings**.

They all have that one common and very powerful bond -- they care deeply about children. And, because they are all new at this huge and very important undertaking, they are very willing to give and receive helpful information.

They share everything: pediatricians, bargains for clothes, food, and friends. They share school experiences and daycare centers. Anything they can share, they share. This is truly the master's class in networking, or even the PhD.

When I was in college, I had someone tell me, make all the lifelong friends you can in school, because when you get your career going, you will not have the time or the common interest with people to make them. Yes, that is somewhat true. However, I have many hobbies and interests, so I have made many incredibly close friends as a professional adult as well. And, if I can do it, you can do it, too.

12
Break Through Barriers to Your Success

We all have barriers or blocks to our success. Once we break those walls down and overcome them, then our whole world changes.

Most successful people have gone through many false starts to overcome the barriers that have stopped them, or else they were lucky. There are often barriers to successful job hunting when you set out to land your dream job. Becoming successful at anything takes determination and practice.

Any accomplished athlete or competitor will tell you that so many of the barriers we experience are in our head. And, being successful at anything takes practice. The skills you are learning in this book may or may not be natural for you. Regardless, continue to practice and get better and better at it. I can take all the tennis lessons in the world, and I will never be Roger Federer. But with lessons and practice, I will be a better tennis player than if I had not taken any lessons or done any practice at all.

It is now time to break down your walls, and develop new skills. What you will learn and get good at in networking will not only help you get your dream job, it also will help you succeed in other areas of your life for the rest of your life. It will help you whenever you need a resource for anything (like my Sea Ray) and potentially will help you get raises and promotions. Keep in mind that moving up is not always with your same company. Sometimes you must move to another company to get that promotion and salary increase. Having a well-established network is like a well-oiled machine and will make any job search or career change much smoother.

The Cycle of Being Laid Off

If you are like the majority of people, it is uncomfortable for you to reach out to people, especially when you have been laid off. First, it is heartbreaking and stunning. You've done your best, and never expected this as a result for your efforts and good work.

Then you think, *It will not take me long to get a new job,* so you take advantage of some time off. You do not want to tell anyone you've been laid off because you think it is embarrassing or none of their business. You tell yourself, *I'll find a job soon enough, and then I will share with them my good news.*

After a while of not finding a job, you start to worry. There are bills to pay and no money coming in, so you stay home to stop spending money. You sit at your computer all day, endlessly looking for openings on websites like Monster.com. You are frantically tweaking and sending out your resume to anything remotely close to what you want. The more resumes you email and upload without any response, the more dejected and upset you feel.

Finally, fear and panic starts to take hold. Money is tight, and nothing is working. You are isolated and not connecting with anyone, which is exactly the opposite of what someone out of a job should be doing, and you know it. And, this is all very normal and standard. If you are at any stage of that cycle now, then I urge you to stop, breathe, and change what you are doing immediately.

One of the most important things you need to know about networking is that asking for help is not about you. It is about the other person.

Let me illustrate my point by putting the shoe on the other foot. Let's say you have a friend or cousin who you like and care about, who is out of work. He has gone months without telling you he has lost his job, and then you find out from someone else that he hasn't worked in months. How would you feel?

You might be hurt that he didn't trust you enough to tell you, especially when he was perfectly okay letting this other person know. You might be frustrated knowing you could have helped, but you were not given a chance. You might be angry that instead of giving you a chance to help, he chose to spiral downward, and now it is affecting his family. In fact, you might even begin to question how close of friends you really are, or if you really ever were as close as you thought.

Now, go back to being that friend or cousin, and in your mind, you are thinking, *We are great friends! I just did not want to impose on you or concern you.*

But, it is too late.

Now, you see that *not* letting your friends and/or family

know you are needing help making connections, weakens your relationship; it does not strengthen it. (Which is what you were wanting to avoid by not imposing. Only in reality, you did the just opposite.)

We are blessed to live in an amazing society where people go out of their way every day to help others. Look at all the nonprofit organizations and all the volunteers. In every city, in every country, people give of their time and their money to help those who are less fortunate. So, it is categorically not true that you will be imposing.

You will be empowering your friends and family to help you, and in the process, making your relationships stronger. People get a great deal of satisfaction in knowing they helped someone close to them. If you don't believe it, just listen to someone who introduced a man or woman to his or her spouse. They brag for the rest of their lives that they are the one who set them up.

Some People Do Not Help

There are three types of people: Those who can help you and will; those who would love to help you and truly do not know anyone, and those who can help you and will not.

Some people will not help, and it is not because of the kind of person you are, it is because they just do not help others. It does not make them a bad person or a selfish person; it usually is because they referred someone in the past, and it blew up in their face or went south, so they made a decision to never do that again.

For example, when my friend needed a shower built in his guest bedroom, I recommended he call my favorite handyman. My handyman was someone who I loved to work with, and he had worked on our house for years. This handyman is the kind of guy that no matter what needed fixing, I could call him, and he could do it. He didn't always show up on time or finish the job when he said it would get finished, but he was honest, and his work was good.

Well, using my handyman did not turn out well for my friend at all. My handyman did a terrible job; the shower was slanted and after months of never correcting it, he stopped returning their phone calls altogether. They finally had to get another guy to come out and tear out the bottom of the shower and tear down the wall to get it right. What had not been done right by my handyman in over three months, was done correctly by this new guy in 10 days.

Every time I saw my friend during his three months of pure frustration, all he would talk about is how this guy would not return his phone calls and how miserable his work was. It made me feel awful. It kind of made me feel like I did not want to risk referring anyone to my close friends ever again. Well, for some people, one bad referral like that, and they will never refer anyone again.

So, if you meet someone like that, remember that it is not about you. It is about their own bad past experience. Of course, people are too polite to come out and say, *Hey, you're a great guy, and I know the COO of the company that would be perfect for you, but guess what? I will never help you because I just do not help people anymore.*

We could only be so lucky to get someone that direct. If they were that forward, we could cross them off our list and put our attention on someone else for their sake and ours.

But, people do not say that.

So, how do you quickly find out if they are the type of person to refer when they can? Well, you can ask for any type of simple referral. Ask them if they know a good handyman, realtor, dentist, or_____ (fill in the blank) who they would recommend. You could ask if they have a good lawn service they would recommend as your lawn guy retired. If they immediately say no without an explanation, then they just are not connectors.

Connectors are people who love to connect people who can help each other. There are some people who love to connect people and some who do not -- no matter what. Remember this is not about you. It is all about how they operate. The sooner you identify the type of person they are, the sooner you can start using your time and emotional capital efficiently.

I use the term *emotional capital* because for many of us, sitting with someone pouring our heart out, hoping to get a referral that will lead to a great interview, only to come up blank, is very deflating. The sooner in the conversation, you can determine if the person you are having coffee with is a connector or not, the better. If they are not a connector, then politely have your coffee, and move on. Or, you can stay and use this time for practice.

Here Is Where the Fun Starts

You know they will never connect you, so you can practice your social networking skills with no risk. You can talk about their family, tell them how much you really admire their _____ (fill in the blank), and have fun warming them up.

See how good you can get at connecting with them and making them feel good. When you do your job right, they will leave thinking you're a really great person, and you will leave feeling more confident in your networking. You had no expectation of getting a referral from the early beginning, and you made them feel really good about themselves. This is your goal in every networking one-on-one exchange.

Consider yourself successful when the person across from you leaves feeling really good about themselves and you. And, you leave feeling very inspired about what they are all about. This cannot be corny; it must be heartfelt. Can you now see why there is no point in sitting down with someone you do not like?

Action Step #3:
Add a Column for Where You Met

Once you write down in Column C what you have in common with each person, go ahead in Column D and write down the place you met them.

This might come up in the first conversation or when you call them to set the first meeting. They might not remember the brief exchange you had at Habitat for Humanity or the art exhibit as an example. It will be helpful to getting that first meeting, when you can gently remind them where and when you met.

In Column E, type in when you want to call each person.

You cannot make 100 phone calls in a day. Space it out. You might be comfortable making eight phone calls a day to set up meetings or you might be comfortable making only four calls a day. Or, you might really want that $50 million dollars quickly, so you are ready to make 10 calls a day to get what you want. That is your personal choice. Whatever you decide, be consistent and stick to it.

See the example on the next page.

The Power Networking Strategy™

Personal Connections

Phone Number	Common Interest	How We Met	When to Call
23-456-7890	chess	Met at the ABC Conference	25-Jun
34-567-8901	fishing	McKinney networking group	15-Jun
45-678-9012	IT	We both worked at Baylor	15-Jun
56-789-0123	We both have kids.	McKinney networking group	14-Jun
67-890-1234	investments	McKinney networking group	13-Jun
78-901-2345	guido's pizza	XYZ Company	12-Jun
89-012-3456	LinkedIn	TUV International	12-Jun
...	...	...	...

PAGE FOR NOTES

13
Make All Your Follow-up Calls

Be realistic and go with what feels best, so you do not get frustrated with the process.

When you call them, they will either be willing to meet with you or not meet with you. If they are willing, you might set a meeting right then and there. If not, they might want you to call back in a few weeks as they are either traveling soon or busy with family or work projects.

In Column F, you will put down when they want a call back. This is most critical because when you call someone, and they put you off to another time, you must call them back when they asked to be called back. This will let them know you are serious and sincere. If you do not call back when that person asked to be called back, you will be dismissed immediately as someone who cannot be relied upon.

Never miss that follow up phone call date.

Nothing sends a stronger, more impressive message to someone than when you follow up on the date they asked you to. Even if they were just putting you off, when you call them back when you said you would, they now have the impression, *this person is serious, on the ball and it would not be a waste of my time to meet with them.*

You might be put off three or four times. But, when you

call them each time when they said for you to call them, they will be very impressed. This is all to get that first meeting. Now, once you get that first meeting, here is where the fun begins. So, let's dissect that first meeting:

First and foremost, you must be positive about everything!

Remember you are always on stage. Negativity is a turnoff, especially in that first meeting. Preparing for this first meeting is vitally important. This is where any elevator pitch you have ever been taught, should be thrown out the window. The person you are sitting with will never care about what you do. If you build microchips and you are meeting with a CPA, he or she probably would not even understand what building microchips is anyway. You do not need the CPA to understand what you do, you need him or her to connect you with someone you want to meet with.

Being a financial advisor has been a wonderful career, meeting many successful people from many different types of businesses and careers. One thing I can tell you is that successful people all have one thing in common: at some point in their lives, they found out what it is they wanted to do, and went for it.

Take Sam Walton for instance. I never worked with him, but he was already 44 years old when he opened his first official Walmart. He was with Ben Franklin Retail for 20 years before that, and he wanted Ben Franklin Retail to go into rural towns. They would not do it. So, he borrowed money to start his first store in Arkansas, and the rest is history. He knew what he wanted, and he went for it.

**The most important thing you can do for yourself
to springboard your life in the direction you desire
is to find out what it is you are really suited to do,
then make sure you are doing that!**

When you are sitting down with someone to help you, the more you can articulate what it is you want to do and how this person can help you, the more successful you will be in getting what you want.

Nothing can kill the exchange faster than when someone asks, "How can I help you?"

And you say, "I am not really sure. But, I am looking to get back to work. Do you know anyone hiring?"

That is total disaster both for you and for the other person. You need to be able to help that person help you. The more you can do that, the closer you will be to getting where you want to go.

In my first accounting class, the instructor walked into the room and laid it all out on the line for us in the opening class. He told us that accounting would have its own language, and it will seem very strange. We would have to learn about depreciation debits, credits, shareholder's equity and many other terms.

He said, "The best way I can make this easier for you is to illustrate this point: If I tell you to go down the hall and open the door on the right, pick up a book and take it three more doors on the left, exchange it for a pencil, then go upstairs and on the first door on the left is piece of paper. Take it off the door and walk down the hallway past five doors... somewhere along there, you are going to give up and tune me out."

"You will never do what I had just asked you to do. But, if I told you, if you follow these EXACT instructions, you will get an automatic "A" in this class, you will listen to every word intensely."

I learned a lot from that opening class.

I learned if you want someone to do something for you, then you need to let them know exactly why you are asking them to do it, and what the endgame is. This will help that person you are sitting across from help you. Of course, he told us the benefit of knowing accounting is in running your own business or helping other business owners run their companies more effectively. In fact, he said, "Understanding accounting can help you in ways you cannot even imagine sitting here today. It is the cornerstone of all business management."

With those words, I fell in love with accounting and majored in it. I was never a good accountant, but I use my accounting degree daily as a successful financial advisor.

Action Step #4:
Add in Your Call Back and Meeting Times.

When you call people, if they ask you to call back at another time, add that date in Column G

This is critical because when you call someone and they put you off to another time, you must call them back when they asked to be called back. It shows you are serious.

If they want to set up a date to meet, add that date in Column G

This is very important for many reasons, but the biggest reason for sure is you do not want to miss the date, time or place. This could be your golden opportunity.

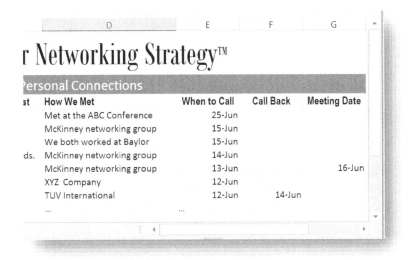

Add your meeting dates to a calendar so you are reminded

when you are going to meet. Follow up is critical in professional networking.

14

Prepare for a Successful Meeting

There is a lot that goes into being prepared for a successful one-on-one meeting. And the follow up is equally important.

When you are wanting to get back into the workforce and get your dream job, then you must do some homework. Let's assume you have done everything I have talked about so far. You have your passions written down, and you now know exactly what you want to do. Now, it is time to figure out what companies would be ideal for you. So, do your homework. Find out about the companies you want to work for. You have so much technology at your fingertips to find all kinds of information.

Identify Your Ideal Companies

Look at all the companies in your wheel space. Make a list of the ones that you really would like to work for. Write them down. Let's say you come up with 10 companies. In your worksheet, next to the person you are going to meet, in the next column after you have put down the date you are going to meet, write down the names of two or three companies you would like to ask this person about. Ask if they know someone in any of those companies you might be able to talk to about working there. This is huge.

Compare this to what most people do. Let's say they are a stress engineer in building bridges. And now, they are sitting down with someone they met at Habitat for Humanity who knows nothing about engineering. They do what they are told to do and give their elevator speech at a coffee with this person and say, "Do you know anyone in any company who needs a stress engineer?" I think you pretty much can imagine the blank stare they are going to get.

This person probably doesn't even know what a stress engineer really does, and most likely has even less of an idea what companies hire stress engineers. So, the effort they spent to arrange this one-on-one is wasted right then and there.

Now, when you say, "I have made a list of companies that I would really like to work for. My passion is helping build solid structures. I have looked at a lot of companies, and a few really stand out as a cut above. Do you know anyone who works at any level for one of these companies?" They might not know one single engineer in any company, but their best friend might be the HR director of one of the companies you mention. Now, they can help you. If you hadn't mentioned the company name, they probably would not have connected the dots to see that they could help.

Do you see how powerful this is?

But until now, you have not given them a clear roadmap as to how to help you. You always want to help the person help you by being prepared and preparing them for the opportunity to serve. We all love to help, right?

Know What You Are Seeking

I am forever reminded of friend who called me one day and asked me to help his nephew get a job now that he was graduating from college. I said, "Sure, have him call me and set a time to come in. I don't know what he wants to do or if I can help, but of course, I will meet with him."

He came in and from the first minute I met him, I knew this kid was ready. He had a passion for real estate appraisal. He had his degree in commercial real estate, and he had specialized in appraisal. I had been a financial advisor for almost 30 years and had worked with people in every profession, but this was a new one for me. I didn't even know you could get a degree in commercial real estate, much less specialize in appraisal.

I was intrigued from the onset. I asked how in the world he got into that. He said from the time he was a kid, he was always fascinated by how much buildings must have cost around him. Now, I was hooked. How often do kids come out of college doing exactly what they have wanted to do since childhood?

However, I was stumped.

I didn't know anyone who did commercial real estate appraisals. And clearly, I had no idea what firms hired them, I asked him if he knew any companies that he would want to work for. He was not sure. He had not taken any of my workshops and was not prepared for that question. But I wanted to help him; he was an awesome young man, mature beyond his years. He truly was focused on where he was going in life. I loved that.

I happened to be sitting on the board of a nonprofit with

a very successful commercial real estate broker. I picked up the phone and called him while the young man was still in my office. I asked him if he knew any firms that hired appraisers. To my surprise he said, "We have a large real estate appraisal department." I had no idea. He said, "Let me go talk with the director and see if he will meet your young man. If you are that impressed with him, he must be special. I will see what I can do."

The young man and I continued talking for few minutes with me coaching him a little bit when the commercial real estate broker called back. He said, "I spoke with the director. He told me he knows you well, and that you should call him directly." Now, I was stunned, I didn't know I knew anyone who did commercial real estate appraisal.

I asked, "Who is that?" When he told me, I couldn't believe it. I had worked on a few boards with the director over the past 20 years. But, it had never come up in conversations as to what he does. So, I called him right away and told him about this kid. He agreed to meet with him. They hit it off right away, and he hired him. Now, this is very rare. Most people aren't going to do all that for you. I just got very lucky that day. Or, perhaps it was this kid's lucky day.

> **"Luck is what happens when preparation meets opportunity."-- Seneca**

Clearly, it would have been much more productive if the young man had told me that he had done his research and these are the biggest companies in the area with appraisal departments. He could have started with, *Do you know anyone in these companies?*

It was luck and sheer determination on my part that I could help him. So being prepared for the meeting is critical. Like I said earlier, only mention two or three companies. This is important. If you list a string of 10 companies you want to work for at the first meeting, then you don't have a reason to follow-up. And the person may wonder if you really want to work for a specific company or just any company that will hire you. If he knows someone at one of these companies, and calls them, it will be a great conversation. It will go like this.

I really want to help this guy that I met at Habitat. He is not working right now, but he is a stress engineer and mentioned your company as the ideal company he wants to work for. Is there someone there you know who will meet with this guy? That is much more powerful conversation, and it always goes back to helping someone help you. Make it as easy on your Advocate as possible.

This kid made it easy for me to want to help him because he was passionate, so I could convey that in the conversation. Remember, the other (and very important) part of not giving the entire list is to give you a reason for follow-up.

Always send a thank you note after every meeting. Always. Always. This is a cardinal rule.

Before you leave the meeting, you will want to ask some key questions: One question you must ask is, "If I come up with some other companies, do you mind if I call you and see if you know anyone in any of them?"

Of course, they will say, "Please do."

Then you can add, "And, by the way. Is there someone you might know who I can reach out to today who might know someone in one of these companies? I would appreciate any help you can give me."

Or this, "Are you close to your CPA, attorney or anyone who might know someone who can get me into one of these companies?"

Keep in mind, this kid reached out to his uncle, who reached out to me. And, he got his dream job. He is still there years later and has had many promotions along the way.

Finally, if he gives you some names, be prepared to write them down. And follow up with this person to make that connection for you. You are always looking to expand your network. Always.

Now, when you put that person he recommended on your worksheet, note whether you will call him or he will call for you (either way is okay). It is always easier and more effective if he calls and makes the introduction on your behalf.

Practice at Home

At first, these few questions will seem awkward to ask. Part of the preparation for these types of meetings will be to practice at home. Sit down with a family member or friend and role play. Remember you are always on stage.

The most celebrated actors of our time didn't go on stage unrehearsed. They practiced every line, in every scene, until they became their character. You must do the same. Only it will be harder for you because this is new for you.

For many, networking one-on-one will be a totally new concept. When you get comfortable with networking, it will change your life. I had no idea how to network when I started my business, and I've practiced mastering networking over the years. I have learned a little bit here and a little bit there. I have constantly practiced, and over time it has become natural for me.

Practice at home and in real life situations. Each time you do this, it will be easier. When you land that dream job, you will feel so empowered. You will understand that you now can do anything that you want to do. Your life will change.

PAGE FOR NOTES

15

Make the Connection

First, the key is to be passionate, caring, and self-confident. Second, keep in mind that most people want to help people who they feel genuinely like them. These are the keys to a successful interchange.

Remember, you are on stage. Practice telling people what you like about them. Connect with people who have the same passions you do. Make sure the opening conversation is all about them. Steer the conversation about what you have in common and what you admire about them. And thank him or her for taking the time to meet with you.

Pay Close Attention

Watch their body language as you progress in conversation. When you are having coffee, pay close attention to see if they are drinking when you drink. It is a little-known trick to determine if they are comfortable with you or not. When you are talking with someone and you pause to drink some of your coffee and they do not, that signals they are uncomfortable with this conversation.

The more relaxed people are in a meeting, the more they will eat or drink. The more uncomfortable the less they will eat or drink. There are books on body language. If you haven't read any of them, you might want to get a couple and check them out. You can get them at any library. Believe it or not, people under stress do not eat or drink much in public. They will do that when they are alone. If you see things are not going well, you need to slow down, take a deep breath, be more conversational and see if you can help this person become more comfortable with you. If you can't, you can't.

Remember there are people who just do not like being connectors. So, practice and move on.

If you are not employed and need to get back to work as soon as possible, you need to build your network and use your time wisely. You cannot spend much money, and you must not sit in an isolated house all day. Isolating yourself will cause you tremendous downward spiraling and extreme stress. You will feel disconnected, alone and afraid. So, keep getting out there and find those people who you really connect with.

Opening the Conversation

Now that you are ready to meet someone for the first time, remember that the conversation should center around a few basic principles. The person you are going to talk to may or may not be willing to help you. If this person does not offer any help, it is not about you. It is just their own personality and past experiences. Remember this conversation is not about you. Also, he or she is not really interested in your past or any negative feelings you are carrying around. Keep it positive.

Keep in mind that if you are sitting with someone who does not have any knowledge regarding your specific skill set, you should not talk much about what it is you do or have done. Center your conversation around the companies you want to work for. So, here is a sample dialogue of how this conversation might go. I am including this so that you will have some idea of how to open this conversation. It is very important to realize that each person reading this book will have a different approach to this, just as each actor plays a character with his or her own personality.

Take this example as an example only.

Start with What You Have in Common

So, now that you are meeting someone for the first time, remember your spreadsheet and what you have prepared for this meeting. Also, remember that people are more likely to help you if they feel a connection with you. This is done by making sure there is something you and this person have in common. It can be a common passion for a hobby, knowing the same person that you both like, or being a family member. Whatever the common link is, open up the conversation with that. It is common ground and a comfortable place to start a conversation.

Have you ever met someone, and they say, "I am from such and such town?"

And you ask, "What high school did you go to there?" And, when they tell you, it just so happens that you have a friend who went to that same high school.

So, you ask if they know your friend, and they say, "Well, yes, I do," and now you have something fun to talk about to a total stranger. Whether you realize it or not, you have just established a common ground to start a conversation with a total stranger. And all the sudden, it becomes a comfortable conversation.

Remember on your worksheet, you have put down what the common bond is between you and the person you are meeting. And, you have put down what you admire and/or like about this person. Make sure you use this and open the conversation with what you have in common. Be sure and make it genuine and not fake.

So, this is how this conversation might go:

Imagine you are meeting at a local coffee house or breakfast café for a bagel and some coffee.

"Hi, Jim, I really appreciate you taking some time to meet me. When we met at Habitat for Humanity, I was very impressed with how well you knew exactly what you were doing. I haven't done much of that myself, but I loved it. Tell me, how long you have been volunteering for Habitat."

(Let them talk and pay attention to what they are saying.) Their answer will lead to more dialogue about how they got started, what they like about it and why they love doing it. If it doesn't progress naturally, ask those questions. It is here that you can also ask if they might know a good lawn person or electrician or something generic. This will help you know if they are a connector of people or not. (I talked about this earlier in the book.)

Once you have exhausted that part of the conversation, it would be okay to say something like, "Are there any other organizations you volunteer your time to like this?"

"Can you tell me about them?" (Again, let them talk.)

Once they have answered all these questions, and you feel they are connector, then it is okay to say something like, "That is so impressive to me. I really admire you for giving so much back to the community. That is one of the reasons I asked you to spend some time with me. I was very impressed with you, and I wondered if you might be able to steer me in the right direction."

"It looks like you know a lot of people. Do you mind if I tell you a little about my current situation? You might be able to help me." (It is important that you ask for permission to change the subject and ask for help. This gets their buy-in that it is okay for you to ask for help and allows this person to change comfortably to second phase of the conversation.) It will also make it more comfortable for you to move forward in the conversation. You won't feel like you are just changing directions in an awkward manner.

Now, the person will say something like, "Sure, what's up?" Or, "How can I help you?" Or, "I will certainly help if I can."

Your answer might be, "I am hoping to get back to work as soon as possible. I loved working for XYZ company and loved what I did for them. I was an ABC for them. There are a few companies in the area I have researched, where I would love to work. I wonder if you know anyone in these companies who I might talk with to see if they have any openings?" Now, name the companies.

The person may or may not know of anyone. However, if they do, you just hit the jackpot! So, you say, "Wow, that is perfect! I would love to meet him/her. Do you mind making an introduction? I would appreciate that so much."

If this person is a connector, they will be more than

happy to make that call. Now you can say something like, "I really would appreciate it. I don't want to impose on you, so when would be a good time for me to check back with you and see if you have had a chance to call her?" This establishes a timeline and lets the person know you are serious about wanting to get back into the workforce as soon as possible.

Now, if this person doesn't know anyone in any of the companies you mentioned, thank them for their interest and time and be very complimentary that they took the time for you to get to know them better.

Then ask, "Do you mind if I stay in touch with you? I am always hearing about other companies that interest me. Do you mind if I shoot you a message or call you to see if you know someone in one of those companies? Of course, they will say, "Sure. Call me anytime."

Then you should add, "If you come across anyone who might know someone in any of these companies or hear of any openings in my field, please keep me in mind. I am anxious to get back to work as soon as possible, and I would really appreciate any help you can give me."

End the conversation here.

If you are meeting someone you have worked with in the past, the conversation is much easier as you have a lot to catch up on. If you are meeting someone who is in your same field but you have not worked with them before, it is also a lot easier to have this conversation. You have a lot of common experiences as you both do the same thing.

16
Keep It Professional

Even in traditional business settings business intentions can get mistaken for personal intentions.

A woman at one of my workshops recently shared her concern that she would feel very uncomfortable asking a man to have a follow up lunch or cup of coffee, simply because her interest in getting together to network might be mistaken for personal interest, especially if she met him at an event where they had mutual interests such as an art appreciation meeting. She would not want to risk that he might take it the wrong way and think she was really interested in more personal interaction than professional.

This can be a problem for sure. Most companies now require everyone to go through what is called *sensitivity training in the workforce*. There are certain things that cannot be said to a member of the opposite sex as those could be construed as sexual harassment or completely inappropriate in any workplace setting.

So how does one network with the opposite sex where there is not an HR governing body watching over how one behaves? And, it does not just affect women. I, as a male, have been approached in a professional setting by a woman inviting me to spend time with her in a romantic setting. I wear a wedding ring, and I am very clearly married.

Here are a few suggestions that might help you navigate the waters of networking with the opposite sex. One is that you should always use common sense and trust your gut instinct on what his/her real intention might be. Sometimes you can tell when you meet someone in a networking environment what their real interest is and sometimes you cannot.

One woman I spoke with, told me that if she is not quite sure of someone's intent, she keeps it strictly coffee in a popular business setting. And, if the conversation does go to flirting, she ignores the comment and brings the conversation back on topic until she can gracefully end the engagement. Of course, how you dress can make a big impression on what message you are wanting to send. When you want this to be strictly professional, be as professionally dressed as you can be without looking totally out of place. Wear nothing that would send a signal that you are looking to attract attention from the opposite sex.

Remember, your biggest goal is to make this person an Advocate who is committed to helping you find your ideal job. And, if you do not get any vibes that this person has an alternative agenda, and you want to meet them for lunch, then go for it.

You would think that if you are married and wear a wedding ring, that should keep these off-handed remarks and suggestions from happening, but we all know too well that in society today, for some people that doesn't mean anything.

Another option for a follow up meeting, is to consider inviting a friend to join you who is also looking for a job. This of course will keep it professional and aboveboard. If you are not comfortable asking a friend to join you all the time, another way is to be prepared with a response that is polite, but to the point.

The subtle way to prevent someone from bringing up a desire to see you socially is to open the conversation with what interested you in the event where you both met. (As I have stated, starting with what interests both of you is how you build the connection in the first place.)

The difference here is that you then bring up the fact that your husband or boyfriend would have attended, too, but he was called away on a business meeting. Say something like, normally, he loves to go to these things with me. Men, you can do this, too. This will send a signal that not only are you involved, but you are involved with someone you are very happy with as you both love doing the same things.

If the other person did have a social interest and now knows you will not go there, he or she will either withdraw because there was not any interest in helping you anyway, or they will continue to build the professional relationship that you were interested in building from the beginning.

Meet in a Public Setting During the Day

I highly recommend that you do not agree to meet someone at a bar who you have only met at a networking event or been referred to. Meeting for drinks with someone of your same sex is not a problem, but meeting with someone of the opposite sex at a bar or for dinner lends itself to a greater opportunity for misconstrued intentions.

Meeting for breakfast, meeting for a cup of coffee or meeting for a casual lunch sends a professional message.

Meeting for dinner one-on-one is more social, especially if it is the first or second meeting where you do not really know if this person can or will help you at all in your job search.

Now that you have done everything you can to set the tone and the mood for this to be a professional follow up meeting, what happens if the other person takes the liberty to see if you are interested in something more than professional?

Be prepared for this. Know what it is you are going to say. If you feel this person was never interested in helping you at all, then your response will be sterner than if you feel there is a good chance this person genuinely wants to help you and still can.

(I will not address what you might say if you think the other person is just playing games and never had any intention of helping at all.)

If you feel this is a decent person who is interested in helping you find your dream job, and they took some personal liberties to test the water to see if you are interested in them, then your response might be more restrained. You should craft your own response, and it might go something like this: I am flattered that you are interested in me, but as I mentioned, I am involved/married. Thank you for asking. Again, choose whatever you want to say. The situation will be awkward no matter how you turn this person down, because no matter what, they will feel stupid for asking. Do not forget, they stuck their neck out to ask.

Then you go right back to the reason you asked for the meeting and be complimentary about the person for the reason you asked for the meeting in the first place. Such as, *You know when we met at the symposium, you asked a really good question. Can you tell me what you thought of the answer given by the speaker?* This takes you back to the beginning of the building blocks of what it takes to make this person your Advocate. And believe it or not, he or she might say, I totally respect that you do not want more since you are involved. Not everyone would respond that way.

Now, you are back on track, and it will not come up again. If, however, the other person digs in and ignores your "no" answer, then you revert to the sterner response and move on. This is not going to work for you. Worst case scenario, leave.

I would not avoid these situations completely. Most people will not say anything that would be misconstrued as inappropriate. Most will understand from the beginning that you are job searching, and you are looking to make connections that will benefit your search.

As I've mentioned before, there are lots of reasons people avoid networking. And, most people will not even try. But for the ones who do and master it, life gets a whole lot easier. Do not let the actions of a few keep you from the good that most people want to do, and will do, for you.

Success Stories

Follow your passion to land your dream job, no matter what your age.

Sarah, who taught me that *you're always on stage*, had an idea on how to start a discount coupon book. She did not have much money, but she was determined that this would be her success, and she was passionate about helping families save money when they went out eating or shopping.

She set out to build the most successful discount book she could. She was more successful than she could have ever foreseen. When she sold her company, it provided financial security for her husband and her for the rest of their lives. She was in her late 50's when she started this venture.

Another example of later-in-life success is about a wonderful lady who always wanted to own a gift shop at a hotel. She spent most of her life raising kids and being a loving wife. In the little spare time she had, she would visit gift shops and talk to the owners. She loved gift shops! After all the kids were educated and had moved on, her husband passed away unexpectedly. So, with little else to go on, she set out to fulfill her passion and find out how to become an owner of a hotel gift shop.

Unfortunately, she didn't have a nest egg to purchase a gift shop; she had to think creatively. She decided her only way was to convince the owner of a gift shop to sell her their gift shop with little or no money down. That worked!

This began her entrance into the hotel gift shop world.

She was so excited, and as a result, she turned her first gift shop into a real money-maker. Soon after, other hotels in that same hotel chain started calling her to sell her their gift shops. You see, the occupancy rate went up because travelers loved talking to her, and she excelled at stocking the shelves with exactly what travelers needed. By the time she passed the business down to her kids, she owned six or more gift shops doing millions of dollars annually. She was in her mid-60s when she started this new career.

Knowing what it is you want to do is not always about getting that dream job, it might be about getting you that million-dollar business! In my late 20s, I tried to start the first pet health insurance company in Texas. I knew there was a need for it, but it was not really my passion. I had always wanted to own my own business. I just did not know at that age what my real passion was. I had a college friend who was a dog trainer by hobby. That was his passion.

He quit his salaried job and went into business with me to raise money to start a pet health insurance company. It was the late 70s or early 80s and no one had ever heard of pet health insurance, but we loved the idea. The Texas Department of Insurance was against it, and no matter how much capital we raised, they kept demanding more. Eventually, we quit fighting the system, and the whole idea crumbled. I went on to become a financial advisor, and he went on to found one of the largest dog agility organizations in the United States. His passion was dogs, and he made a very successful company from it. We were ahead of our time on the pet insurance, as it now is a multi-million-dollar industry.

Another example of this is a friend of mine who got her

master's degree in music therapy. She is a great teacher, but just didn't like teaching music in the school environment. So, she went into sales, but that was not what turned her on either. Finally, she went into corporate training. That is what she loved and did until she retired due to company downsizing. She was at a fairly young age and retirement at a young age can be isolating and lonely.

I begged her to start a small, private piano school. I knew she loved the piano and loved teaching. I explained to her that teaching kids privately is nothing like working in a school environment. For years, she refused. Finally, out of sheer boredom, she agreed to try something different. She took on one student to see how things would go.

And then, BINGO! She hit the jackpot! One student quickly became five. Then five became 10; 10 became 20; and now her life is not only teaching kids and adults how to play the piano, but also being surrounded by people who love music all day long. She is forever grateful for my persistence.

17
Reach Out to Special Interest Groups

The more you spend your time volunteering and having fun doing it, the quicker you will get out of that downward cycle you might be in.

Go online and find all the nonprofit organizations, associations or groups that share your passions. You can also go to Meetup.com and find local groups that are looking for people of similar interests. Start a new worksheet and make a complete list of all the groups that interest you. Then contact them and ask when you can meet with them and see what they are all about.

The more you invest your time volunteering and enjoy how you spend your time, the quicker you will meet people who love the same things that you do and feel connected to you because of your shared interests. This will vastly expand your network with the right people. You might even find a job with one of these organizations.

I have worked with many nonprofits. It invariably comes up that someone I am working with got their job because they used to volunteer there. They are so happy. Not only do they have a great job, but they are passionate about their work. This is huge in anyone's life.

Only 10% of our happiness has anything to do with finances. Once our financial needs are met, it is more about doing things that you love to do and being with people who you enjoy being with.

In this new worksheet section, you will make all the similar notes that you did for your other worksheet. Write all of your groups in Column A. And, add the other columns that relate to:
- Who do you contact to meet to get involved?
- When are you going to contact them?
- When is the next meeting?
- What is it about this organization that interests you?

You want to keep track of all of this as you do your homework. When you do this right, you will get very busy, very quickly meeting all the right people. I once did a workshop and someone raised their hand asked, "What do I do if I do not know anyone in town and just moved here?" Well, this section will do it for you. Get involved. Meet people who have your same interests immediately. You will also find you are making new, wonderful friends.

I recently read in the morning paper about a woman who moved to town and didn't know anybody, so she started a support group for women who were new to town. In the age of social media, it has grown very fast and very quickly.

Getting involved with people who share your interests helps so much emotionally, too. You will feel like you are in control of your life again. Getting laid off and not finding an immediate job makes people feel like they have no control over their lives anymore. They start to point fingers at others and themselves. Getting out there and meeting new people with the same interests can do wonders.

When you do this right, you will find you do not have

enough time in the day to do everything you need to do. What used to be a day filled with boredom, searching for jobs online, submitting resume after resume, will now be spent in the real world interacting with real people -- people who can connect you to your dream job.

How to Become Active at a New Organization

Going to any new organization can be a very lonely feeling. Everyone knows everyone, and you do not know anyone yet. You might just go and listen and not talk to anyone. Or you might talk to one or two people briefly. You might feel like going was a total waste of your time. So, there is a way to change all that. Here's how:

Before you go to any new organization to meet people, look on their website. The goal is to find out who is in charge of that organization. If they do not have a website, but there is a leader mentioned to contact for more information, use that. But the goal is find out who is in charge. Then call that person and tell them you are keenly interested in meeting people in their group. And, tell them why. Talk about your common interest in whatever that group is meeting for. Then ask the leader when you can meet prior to going to the meeting, so you will at least know someone before you go. Most leaders of groups or organizations are people oriented and strong connectors. Their sole reason for being a leader is that they love the group and want it to grow.

Once again, remember, it is not about you, it is about the wants and needs of the leader or president of the chapter. Some organizations are very developed and have a president, vice president, etc. When you set up this meeting, and meet, you have a natural conversation point. You might ask, "Tell me about the group and its members. Who do you like and know well? How did you get started, and how long have you been their leader?"

Let them know that you want to come to a meeting and would greatly appreciate some personal introductions to members they think would be a great connection for you. You might even tell them you are looking for job and anyone who can help you in your search would be especially appreciated. Let the leader know the companies you would like to work for and ask if there is anyone who the leader knows in your field or with those companies.

The person or persons who are part of the group that the leader suggests you meet, may not even come to many meetings, so in that case, ask for their contact information. Then, when you call them, let them know that the leader of that group suggested you call because_____.
See if he or she is willing to meet you in person. Now, you have at least one more person on your worksheet to network with. Your network is always evolving. Keep up with it.

But, either way, when you go to your first meeting, you will know the leader and he or she will gladly introduce you as a newcomer and ask everyone to welcome you to the group. Then you also will get lots of attention from anyone you sit next to. They will ask you your background, where you live, all the general questions. That is natural. You will make lots of new acquaintances who have your similar interests and hobbies.

Use this strategy for any new group you want to join and you won't feel awkward or lonely going to that 'first' meeting. You will be amazed at how big your network will get and how much fun you will have meeting people that you connect with instantly.

Networking at Professional Associations

At any professional association's group meeting, you might be asked to stand up and introduce yourself. If it is a nonprofit, speak to your passion for what they are doing. That is why you joined. You need to say that up front. Then you need to say, you are not working right now, and would love to meet personally with anyone who feels they might know someone in a couple of companies you would love to work for.

At that moment, someone might ask out loud what are those companies? Then you should be ready to list them. You need to be ready. Again, practice all this, a lot. Become smooth at this. This is your golden opportunity. If you are not asked what companies you want to work for, do not worry. Someone might come up to you later and say, "Let's get together and see if I can help." Bingo! You just expanded your network.

Some of the building blocks to networking are self-confidence, passion and lots of practice.

Action Step #5:
Create a Similar Worksheet for Special Interests Groups

You are starting to get the flow of networking and creating a list of your potential Advocates.

It will be easy if you open a new worksheet and copy the PERSONAL worksheet into the new worksheet. There you can make changes to the column headings and rearrange as needed. Or, simply download the template at:

www.ThePowerNetworkingStrategy.com

See the example below.

The Power Networking Strategy™

Special Interest Groups

Advocate	Phone Number	Group	Common Interests	When to Call	Call Back
Robert Ross	123-456-7890	Habitat for Humanity	We like pounding nails.	25-Jun	
Lori Frank	234-567-8901	Outdoor Explorers	Love meeting active people.	15-Jun	
Julia Moon	345-678-9012	Art Enthusiasts	I love art shows.	15-Jun	
Sam Smith	456-789-0123	Fishing Experts	I love to fish.	14-Jun	
Ali McGregor	567-890-1234	How to Sew	I want to learn how to sew.	13-Jun	
Julie Morgan	678-901-2345	Basket Weaving	I want to do something creative.	12-Jun	
Sophia Morales	789-012-3456	Chess Club	I played chess as a kid. I would like to get better	12-Jun	14-J

Personal | Special Interest Groups | Professional Associations | Career Support Groups

18
Add Professional Associations and Advocates

Whatever your skillset, there are organizations in almost every city that will have your profession as the focal point of a group.

You may have only one profession you are interested in, or you may be considering two or three professions. Create a Professional Associations worksheet for each of the professions you are considering. Here are the real innerworkings of networking. I cannot emphasize enough the importance of this section(s).

This section is very different and must be treated very differently than anything we have talked about so far. Here is where you can really be yourself and relax. You will meet people who not only have your passion, but also do what it is you want to do. (See notes on worksheet.)

They might even have the job that you want to have. Maybe you are not working right now, or maybe you are and you want to change to something else. Sometimes you need to reinvent yourself. Many people in life have.

You might even invest your free time taking courses to learn more about what you really want to do. Maybe you need special licenses or certifications. When you start going to these meetings, you need to know your goals before going.

When you are wanting to change your profession and need to reinvent yourself, your objective is to meet successful people in that profession to get all your questions answered. And again, you will meet people to put on your networking list.

When you meet with them, you are wanting information. You might want to know what courses you should be taking, where to take them, what is it like working at this type of job? What did they do to become successful? Who should I know in this field? Who should I talk to?

If you are unemployed and going to these meetings to get back into the workforce in the same skill set or profession, you will want to build your network with people already working in your endeavor. This is huge and will shorten your search.

Some of these professional associations even have an opening in their meeting for those who are not working and want to. You are given the opportunity to stand up and talk about yourself. This is tricky. In most of my workshops, I ask someone to stand up and talk about themselves and what they are looking for. Often, people cannot do that concisely and meaningfully. They stumble and reduce their chances of getting someone who can help them.

So, before you go to any association meeting, nonprofit meeting or networking meeting you need to practice what it is you want to say expecting you are going to be asked to stand up and talk quickly and precisely.

Keep your elevator pitch to 30 to 60 seconds.

The worst thing is to be faced with the opportunity to

stand up and talk about yourself and you freeze. That will be a golden opportunity wasted.

You will want to have different pitches prepared for different types of organizations. You will want to tell them why you are there or why you have joined. If you are at a meeting with professionals doing what you do, then you can use your elevator speech.

Informational Interviews

What is an informational interview? An informational interview is an informal conversation with someone working in an area that interests you. They should be able to give you information and advice. It is an effective research tool in addition to reading books, conducting online searches and attending workshops and support groups.

A couple of pointers to remember during the informational interview: 1) You must always be on stage and ready to subtly sell yourself. 2) Always ask for specific help during the informational interview. Otherwise, you will miss out on a major opportunity.

Please make sure you turn this "informational interview" into a networking opportunity. Once you have spent time with this individual, either on the phone, at a workshop, or having coffee, do not be shy about taking it one step further.

Ask if they have any other contacts in your field of interest who would be willing to help you a bit further in your job search. Ask if they are in any position to get you to the person who hires in either the company where they work or any of the other targeted companies on your list. Have a piece of paper and a pen or pencil ready so you can write down their answers as they talk. Don't make them wait while you get this, and do not make them repeat themselves.

Action Step #6:
Create a Similar Worksheet(s) for Professional Associations

You are starting to get the flow of networking and creating a list of your potential Advocates.

Now you can create a worksheet for each of your PROFESSIONAL ASSOCIATIONS the same way you did your SPECIAL INTERESTS GROUPS worksheet.

See the example below.

The Power Networking Strategy™

Professional Associations

Phone Number	Group	Common Interest	When to Call	Call Back	Meeting Date
4-567-8901	Database Management	President of Group	15-Jun		
5-678-9012	Hospital IT Professionals	Connection to Scott White.	15-Jun		
6-789-0123	DFW IT Professionals	President of the State Organization	14-Jun		
7-890-1234	Fort Worth IT Professionals		13-Jun		16-Jun
8-901-2345	Meetup for IT Pros	Group Leader	12-Jun		
9-012-3456	Chess Club		12-Jun	14-Jun	
3-456-7890	Dallas IT Professionals	Both worked at Baylor Hospital in 1980	25-Jun		

Special Interest Groups | Professional Associations

PAGE FOR NOTES

19
Prepare Your Elevator Pitch

When you are in a professional association where everyone does what you love to do, then your pitch is very different.

Here you are talking with people who know what it is you want to do. When you get up and speak here, you can let loose. You should go into exactly what you have done, what you loved about it, and what it is you want to do. It is here that you can let people know some of the companies you would like to work for.

When you are lucky, someone there will currently work for one of the companies you are seeking. That will be a huge win for you. If you don't experience that, it's okay. Give out your contact information right then and there. This is the only time you should do that.

Say to the group, "If any of you know someone I should contact, feel free to call me anytime." Then work strategically to meet individuals and get their contact information after the meeting as well. Some might even ask for a copy of your resume. That is the golden offer. Get their contact information right then and there. And, follow up quickly.

These are very different presentations, and you must be prepared. You cannot stumble around and be awkward. You want to be smooth and confident and above all else, do not act desperate.

You can learn a lot from these different types of situations. When you meet with these people, don't just focus on the organizations you have targeted. These people have friends in your profession in lots of companies. They know who is happy and who is not.

You might have targeted a company only to hear from one of these people that their friend hated it there and why. Now everyone is different and what is not a fit for one might be a great fit for another. So, listen and make up your own mind as to whether or not that company is a good fit for you.

Or you might get just the opposite, and they may say, I have a friend who loves working for XYZ Company and you may not have even thought about that company or known they had a division that did what you love to do.

The big deal here is anyone in your profession who is working, also generally knows who is hiring and who you should call. When you have done everything on point, then you will have made this person your Advocate and they will go out of their way to get you in.

If you are not comfortable in one-on-one conversations, remember, it is not about you. It is about making the other person comfortable by letting them know what you have in common and what you admire about them. It will be on your worksheet. Be prepared.

If you are not comfortable speaking in public, practice at home what you want to say. Or even join a local Toastmasters group. There you can meet others who are uncomfortable and want practice, too. If you are not currently working, you have lots of time to really get good at this. Take advantage of this. When you get good at this, you will find your life so much easier when you want anything personally or professionally. You will have a network and be part of a network that will continually be growing.

When you are very lucky, you will get your dream job and someone in your network will reach out to you for help. And then you will help someone else get what they want out of life with the network you have set up. This is the ultimate reward. I know from personal experience.

PAGE FOR NOTES

20
Attend Career Support Groups

Support groups for people who are unemployed are generally hosted by local churches or social service nonprofit organizations.

In almost every community, there are nonprofit organizations that offer support groups to help people who are in transition. Sometimes these are your local churches and sometimes these are community service organizations. Seek them out. Go to several, not just one. Each has different speakers that give good ideas on how to improve your chances of landing that dream job you deserve to land.

There are also city and state sponsored unemployment offices that offer counseling. Visit these as well. The sooner you get in gear and get all the resources available working for you, the sooner you will get back to work doing something you really want to do. This is how you position yourself for success.

Again, Be Prepared and Connect

At these support group meetings, you definitely will be asked to stand up and say what you are looking for. It is great practice. You do not want to get too specific about what you do. However, there may be a few people there who know about your particular job and its requirements. They may also be in the same field. This will be a common bond and goes on your networking sheet.

**Make sure you say the companies
you would love to work for.**

Anyone in any group might know someone in the company you are targeting. They will either say it right then and there or approach you afterwards. Get their information and follow up.

These groups have great speakers who can teach you how to make your resume stand out and how to use LinkedIn to your advantage. We live in amazing times. The current technology allows us to connect with people like never before. Learn how to use all your resources. You have Facebook, Twitter, LinkedIn and so many ways to stay in touch and connect with people today. Reach out to them and tell them what you like and appreciate about them. Use the same strategies that you would use to connect with people in person.

Action Step #7:
Create a Similar Worksheet for Career Support Groups

Now create a worksheet for your CAREER SUPPORT GROUPS the same way you did your other groups.

You will want to make a list of all the support groups in your area and make sure you attend their meetings.

See the example below.

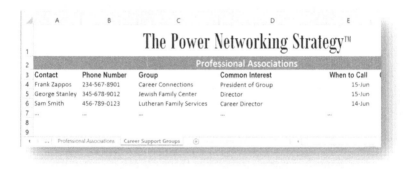

As you are building out your worksheets, you will find that your days will be full. Instead of waking up each morning wondering what you are going to do each day, you will now have almost more than you can get done each day.

Building out your worksheet, meeting new people and going to many different kinds of group meetings will be a full-time job. Instead of sitting at home feeling like a victim, you will now be in charge of creating your future.

PAGE FOR NOTES

21

Remember Past Co-workers

Who is in a better position to refer you than someone you have already worked with? They know you and your work ethic better than anyone.

The last section of your worksheet should be a list of everyone you have ever worked with. Of course, as always, only put down those people who you have enjoyed working with. When I make this point in my workshops, I usually get the same comments from all the groups. The attendees express concern that they have lost touch with their past co-workers. They wonder if it would be awkward to call someone who they have not spoken to in over 10 years. I am absolutely sure that anyone you contact from your past working experiences, whether it was a co-worker, supervisor, someone you supervised, or your boss, will be happy to hear from you, especially if it was a positive relationship.

The main reason you want to make this list is because these people have direct working experience with you. Remember, there are many jobs that are never posted because they are filled by referrals from people within the company. Who is in a better position to refer you than someone you have already worked with? They know you and your work ethics better than anyone. Imagine if there was a job opening in a company where one of your previous work relationships presented your resume to HR with the following recommendation: I worked with this person for a couple of years at XYZ Company and he/she was fantastic to work with. He/she always knew exactly what to do and had a strong work ethic. You would be lucky to get him/her to work here. This will usually seal the deal before you even get interviewed. The job will be yours to lose.

Make a full list on your worksheet of everyone you have ever worked with. It might be hard to find them, but with Facebook, LinkedIn and a bit of other investigative work, you should be able to reach them.

I call this the rifle approach to networking. Once this list on your worksheet is complete, you will now have additional avenues for your job search with more contacts to reach out to. Do not leave one stone unturned. There is a real possibility that someone you have lost contact with is now in a position to help you. Some would call it luck, others might call it *positioning yourself for success*. The end game here is that you could be working with someone you already know and that is a very comfortable feeling.

22

Go Beyond Networking

As soon as you find out you are laid off, there are other avenues to explore. There are some things you should do, and some things you should not do, but I do want to make you aware of what those are.

Once you start networking at these support groups, you will start listening to many speakers. These speakers are usually local experts in your community in a specific field. Some will be experts in LinkedIn and give you some good ideas on how to use LinkedIn more efficiently to network to get that great job that is just around the corner for you.

As you have read over and over in my book, networking is the key to getting where you want to go. And, I encourage you to use all the technology that is available today as well as face-to-face networking. If you see a local group has a speaker lined up for teaching how to use LinkedIn, by all means go and learn.

Please don't ever assume that you know everything there is to know about LinkedIn and other job or people connecting websites. LinkedIn, Facebook, Instagram and others are continually changing and adding features to further connect people with their special interests and communities. There are lots of websites and YouTube tutorials on any subject, so do your research. Keep abreast of all changes and know what is included in your Apple iOS and Android app updates. Fortunately, or unfortunately, technology is running our world so keep up or else you will be left behind.

You might also see that there are speakers that highlight the most effective way to write a resume so yours gets noticed. They will teach the resume killers that definitely will get your resume tossed aside without even being read. Go to these groups and listen and learn from as many different instructors as you can. You will also hear from HR professionals in your community who volunteer their time to speak and talk about what to do and not do when interviewing.

Most of these speakers are professionals in your community who make a living teaching these skills. They will hand out business cards, and you can hire them to be your personal coach. They will personally help you write your resume or teach you how to use LinkedIn or prepare you for an interview. I am sure I have not exhausted the list of what you can learn or who you can meet who will coach you personally.

Some coaches will want to charge by the hour as you use their services. Some will accept payment for the fees you have mounted up after you get your job, as they know you are now unemployed and want to conserve your resources. Not everyone who gets laid off is in desperate financial straits. A lot of people have ample savings and do not mind investing in good coaching.

Some coaches will offer online courses you can invest in and once you take the course, you can get personal coaching for an extra fee. The question you will want to ask at this point is, *Is it worth paying for all that?* How would you know who is credible and can really help you and who can't?

Don't ever think that just because they have been invited to speak, that the nonprofit has vetted them and recommends them as a professional service. Nonprofits are very well intentioned and love to have good speakers for education. This is almost always free of charge to you. But the church or nonprofit is not endorsing this professional, his or her service or the courses they sell. What you do not want to do is spend a lot of money on coaching and end up with poor advice and wasted time and money.

So, how does one know who to work with and who not to work with? I cannot give you the acid test here as everyone who needs help will respond differently to differing coaching. What one coach does really well for one person, might not be what works for you. Some of it will depend on how you relate to the professional and how they listen to you and work with you.

There are a few things you should do before you spend any money with any professional who wants to help you land a great job.

1) Ask if the professional has any books out that you can read. If you can, buy the book and read it. See if the message in the book fits your personality and excites you to want to learn more from the author.
2) Ask what credentials the person has for coaching or teaching the subject. Some professionals are certified and have gone through specific training.

3) Find out what organization certified the individual and how long they have held that certification. If you cannot get the information, that might be a red flag.
4) Check out all the qualifications the person has. Remember, just because the person is a good speaker and speaks to a nonprofit, does not mean they are qualified to charge you a fee for their services.
5) Many use these nonprofits to build their clientele and promote their services and are not just speaking for free to help people in community and give back. Do not get me wrong. There are wonderful people in every community who are very talented and can help you a great deal.
6) Do your research before you sign up for any fee-based training.
7) Ask for referrals of those who have paid the fee and taken their training in the past. Call them. Get their feedback. Ask good questions. Ask what they got out of the training, what they liked and what they didn't like. Ask if they would do it again. If they would, would they do it the same way? Would they change anything as to how they approached the training? Ask if they used anyone else who was helpful to them. Ask what skillset they learned that made the biggest difference. Learn all you can.

After you have done your basic due diligence, sit down with the professional. Talk with him or her about what they see you need to learn and what it will do for you. See if you feel like you will click. Do you like this person? Do you think this person likes you? If all this checks out and you want to take the course or the training, then it might be a good skill for you to learn.

You certainly are not alone in your quest for getting back into the workforce as soon as possible. You have an entire community standing ready to help. There are so many wonderful organizations that work tirelessly to help you. There are so many incredible people who volunteer their time to help you get where you want to go, that you are never alone in your quest.

Your job is to use everything you can and take advantage of everything you can. You just do not want to be taken advantage of in the process by those who see you as desperate and vulnerable.

So, by asking just a few simple questions, you can get on your way and have a smooth and fun journey to changing your life with those who truly care that you do. If you can, see if you can find a mentor who you would really like to discuss things with. This could be a family friend, a priest or any clergy. Before you go in any one direction, call your mentor and run it by him or her. Get some good caring advice. You are not alone. You are part of an incredible community.

Once you have mastered all this and get your dream job, I challenge you to pay it forward to help the next person. You are a person of great talent, great wisdom and lots of experience with plenty to share and give.

Make sure you follow up with everyone you connected to when you finally get your dream job. Some will have had a direct impact on you, and some will not have had any impact at all. But each person who took the time to meet with you or talk with you will care about you. When you get that dream job, send a text, e mail or call everyone to let them know. The more they helped you, the more I urge you to call them. This will let the person know they are not just being used, but you genuinely appreciate all their efforts and it meant a lot to you. If you can, let them know how their efforts helped you specifically, even if it was in some small way.

A perfect way to articulate a thank you is:
"It's friends like you who help make the world a
better place. Thank you so much for your time
and interest in helping me."

A quick thank you goes a long way in keeping that channel of communication open for possible future networking needs

23
What is Failure?

I often work with trainees who seek to become successful Financial Advisors. Many face an initial hurdle of passing various state and federal exams. Each advisor must pass two initial federal exams, the Series 7 and Series 66. Trainees must then pass state exams to allow the soliciting of insurance products as solutions to individual needs.

One such candidate came to me recently, saying she had failed her Series 7. She insisted she had done well in studying the modules and in all practice exams but was stunned to learn she did not pass. "It is impossible to fail the exam," I replied. She asked how I could say that. She explained that upon submitting all of her answers, she was notified almost immediately of her failing grade.

Again, I did not accept this as a true failure. "You didn't fail," I said. "You have not passed yet. You only fail if you quit. You can take it again."

I spent most of the following night reviewing this exchange in my mind, wondering where she had gotten the idea she failed. Finally, it dawned on me. In school, we are given one chance to take an exam, either to receive a passing or failing grade. You can take additional exams to improve your grade, but it doesn't erase the failing grade tied to a specific test. School teaches the concept of failure and reinforces the emotions of having failed. This starts in earlier grades, but lasts well throughout college.

However, life outside of school doesn't work this way.

University entrance exams allow you to submit your best grade after three or more opportunities. You may take professional licensing exams as many times as possible until you pass. I remember taking my Series 7 exam like it was yesterday. People around me asked how many times I had taken it. I said it was my first, and many replied that it was their second, third or even fourth time. States allow lawyers to take the bar exam an unlimited amount of times until they pass. So, where do we get the emotion of having failed? In school.

Something I've learned in this business and in working with successful people is that many were not successful in their younger years. They pursued one opportunity after another until finally something clicked that married their passions with opportunity. Yet, they did not consider it a failure when initial efforts didn't pan out. Most successful people are aware things don't always happen the way they hoped, but this doesn't indicate anything other than a need to try something else to succeed.

Consider a young Tiger Woods, regarded as one of the greatest golfers who ever lived and one of the most famous athletes of all time. He learned early that golf is not a game of great golf shots, it is a game of misses. Golf shots that land out of the open fairway, called the ruff, or land in sand traps. He often said, "It is imperative to learn how to manage the misses."

In baseball, superstar batters hit a .350 batting average. In layman's terms, the best batters in baseball achieve a great hit 35 percent of the time and miss 65 percent of the time. Misses at bat are due to a strike out, fly out, or many other reasons. Top batters receive up to $60 million for being great only 35 percent of the time! They don't think of the other 65 percent as having failed – just as an opportunity to learn for next time.

Getting laid off or fired from a job does not mean you have failed, which is what school leads you to believe. All it means is that the job or company culture wasn't the right fit for you at the time and there are countless more opportunities in store. The world is full of people who didn't fit within the traditional corporate world and went on to start their own successful businesses.

Maybe these first businesses didn't make it, but they kept on until they found a way to fulfill their dreams. Success starts with inspiration, quickly followed by perspiration. Above all else, it requires the inherent belief that you must keep trying until you succeed, and failure cannot be a word in your vocabulary.

I know the feeling well, because it happened to me. I found out early in life that I was not meant for the corporate world as an accountant. Faced with this fact, I was forced to find my own way. At one point or another, we all do.

Doctors change medical groups regularly until they find the right group. Rarely does anyone get their path right the first time, and I have yet to meet anyone who has.

Remember that all the feelings of failure you might experience from losing a job or having a business that doesn't work, you learned in school. The real world gives you the opportunities to keep trying. Imagine the leaders we would create if we gave everyone more chances to take their exams or turn in their papers until they achieved the desired results. Instead, we tell a young eight-year-old he failed.

What a waste.

Why We Don't Network

The most important part of networking is learning to work with others to get your dream job. This means you have to overcome all your current feelings about networking that might be holding you back. As I have mentioned, I speak frequently and hear a litany of reasons why people who have been laid off or are looking to move refuse to network.

Here are a few of the reasons: they are too prideful to ask for help, they feel strongly about not imposing on friends, and a huge number would feel rejected if they asked for help and didn't get the help they asked for. We live with so many self-destructive feelings that we are often paralyzed by them. The feeling of having to do it all by ourselves without the help of others is contrary to the real world.

I would place a large bet that most people include a skill on their resume about working well in teams. Why? The corporate and business world is all team-based, filled with people who collaborate to get a project finished. Yet, everyone has worked with a person who won't share and wants to do everything by themselves. We deem them control freaks. Where does their notion of needing to be in control come from? Furthermore, when did we learn that asking for help is negative?

Again, I reflect back on our days in our classrooms at school. What were we constantly instructed to do? We were taught, not just taught but actually penalized if we asked other students during a test for the right answer. That was called cheating. We were conditioned from the age of four or five that we were to do our own work. While I agree that each person must learn how to think for themselves, learn discipline, and learn how to achieve goals, making that the sole learning process becomes destructive.

There must be a balance between learning how to achieve one's own potential and understanding the benefits and value of teamwork. Unfortunately, I don't feel we were taught that balance. It's no wonder as adults we won't ask for help when we are laid off or fired. We have been conditioned from a young age that we need to succeed without the help of others.

Professional networkers know that success comes more easily when we create the right relationships with the right people. Professional networkers weren't programed by the school system to believe they had to succeed on their own. Successful people never felt failure in school when they didn't get the grade they tried so hard for, because they were either lucky enough or too stubborn to accept those feelings.

In corporate golf outings, a group of four play what is called Best-Ball. The rules are as follows: each player makes a shot, and then the group collectively goes to the best of the four shots to hit the next shot. Often in this scenario, not one of the players on their own could break below 80, and most can't break a hundred. Only 10 percent of golfers can shoot below 100.

In Best-Ball, the group will usually shoot a score between 60 or 70. If you don't play golf, an average course score for 18 holes is around 72. This puts the team score as much as 12 shots below a course score. Professional golfers can do this, but not amateurs.

Together, a group of below average golfers can get a score that mirrors a professional.

Imagine the improvement on school exams if we allowed a group of four to work together on a test. Everyone might receive As, whereas individually, each student might receive a C. While I don't have the research to prove this, I have heard that more progressive schools are letting students learn and take exams together. In fact, in Plano and Mesquite, Texas, there is now a K-12 charter school called Legacy Preparatory Academy that is tuition free. This Academy is project-based learning.

The risk of such an approach is that some students won't do the work and just let others in the team succeed for them. Unfortunately, those types won't do the work on their own either. So many students never reach their potential. It is obvious that working in groups won't fix that, nor will it create a lazy-type student. Even with one or two weak students, I can almost assure you a group will receive higher marks than each individual.

Most projects are team-based in the corporate world. Why don't they consider this more in schools? When students enter graduate school, almost everything is group-based project work. This is because graduate students are being properly prepared for the real corporate world. In summary, networking to land your dream job is all about engaging others.

Life is all about working with others and developing this skill might help you get your dream job. Dr. Robert Arbetter, author of a book on nutrition called *Connecting the Dots*, is also a retired United States Air Force Colonel. He was the U.S. Air Force's Administrator of the Year more than once. He made this point to me, "In the military, one of the strongest recommendations that a person must have to get promoted is to be a team player. In fact, playing alone will get you killed in the field along with everyone else."

Just as it is critical that you not consider setback as failure, it is equally important not to let the conditioning of your past keep you from networking. I would stipulate that in order to be successful in your life, you must do the opposite of everything you were led to believe when it comes to working with others. You must look at success as something you are entitled to have, and in which you cannot fail. Remember, you just haven't succeeded yet. The more people you engage to help you on your journey, the more pride you should have in yourself.

Never Walk Alone

The following lyrics are from the great song, *You Will Never Walk Alone*, featured in Rodgers and Hammerstein's 1945 musical, *Carousel*. This song and its words still ring true today.

When you walk through a storm
Hold your head up high
And don't be afraid of the dark
At the end of a storm
There's a golden sky
And the sweet silver song of a lark
Walk on through the wind
Walk on through the rain
Though your dreams be tossed and blown
Walk on, walk on
With hope in your heart
And you'll never walk alone

It is perfectly natural to feel as if you are walking through a storm right now. If you pay close attention to the song's lyrics, you will see that being in a storm does not signal the end. If you hold your head up high, and walk with hope in your heart, you will never walk alone.

If you feel anxious, revisit this song, it holds a message of hope. My book teaches how to create a network to land your dream job and it carries this same message of hope and the value of never giving up. That is the *Power Networking Strategy and the Personal Approach to Landing Your Dream Job*.

Epilogue
Position Yourself for Success

Taking these action steps, you are going to meet the right people to increase your odds to land your dream job.

You are no longer just sitting around looking at the computer all day or watching TV or sending out job applications online hoping someone will read it. You are getting out meeting the right people who are sincerely interested in helping you find your dream job.

In chess, they say the best defense is a good offense. But there is another byproduct to this whole process that cannot be quantified. I call it, *positioning yourself for success.* If you asked others, they might call it being lucky. Some might say it is just dumb luck when something happens to fall in your lap that you were not expecting.

I remember when I was a young, I was watching a major golf tournament on TV, and one of the top golfers made an incredible 50-foot birdie on the 18th hole to win the tournament. An announcer called it a 'lucky putt.' My dad corrected that statement and told me that when you put in three hours a day, every day, for 15 years, it is not just luck.

Sure, if he tried it 10 more times, he probably would not make it again. But that one time, he did. That's *positioning yourself for success.* When you do all the right things, sometimes everything comes together at just the right time, such as when an actor finally makes it big, they say overnight success took 10 years!

And when it does, it was not anything you were thinking was going to happen. For instance, I know the story of a young man working as an intern in an office hoping to land a job when he graduated college. While working in the office, the receptionist took time off for maternity leave. The office manager asked the intern if he could fill in part-time at the receptionist desk.

Of course, this is not what he wanted to do in the office upon graduating. But, he loved the company. And, because he wanted to show that he was a team player, he agreed to do it. In that position, he met everyone in the office, and everyone got to know him better. As he approached his graduation, he made a list of the different departments that he thought might be a good fit for him. He would talk to those departments to see if they had an opening for him. There was one department that he thought was overstaffed and it was, so he never put that one on his list.

As it turned out, that department had a need he was not aware of as the manager had not discussed it with anyone yet. The team met and decided this young receptionist had the perfect personality for the job and the right educational background. The manager reached out to the receptionist and offered him a full-time position. He was so excited, he took it on the spot. While he never approached them, he got exactly what he wanted by being in the right place at the right time. As a temporary receptionist, he was *positioned for success*.

There are so many stories in the business world of businesses that have grown because they were in a certain industry that got hot, and they were open to opportunities. If you are a real estate buyer, you might buy a piece of land you think is in a good area. However, I doubt you would ever expect that one day someone would want to build a mall across the street and make you independently wealthy as a result of that land purchase. But it happens because you *position yourself for success*.

Landing your dream job is very much like this. When you are networking, adding to your worksheets and talking to people to help you get the job you want, who knows what opportunities might show up that you never would think of on your own.

Be Open to Receiving at All Times

As you are networking and talking with people, you never know what will come from your conversations. You will be *positioning yourself for success*. Be open to it at all times. If you become myopic and only look at what you are trying to achieve with your networking, you might miss the one thing that could change your life. That means, be open mentally and with your heart. To be able to grab opportunities might mean taking risks without knowing the outcomes.

To many people, this sounds impossible. People do not like failure and certainly do not like risk. But the little secret here is that when you want to go where you haven't gone before to get your dream job or dream lifestyle, you need to take some risk. Don't ever feel like you will fail because you took that risk. Read all the false starts I went through before something totally worked for me.

If you're unemployed, you do not want to go back to something you do not like just for a paycheck. You want to have fun in your next job or business you start. You need to take some risks to do that. *Position yourself for success.*

If that young man had said no to the receptionist job, he would have never received the offer from the most prestigious department in the firm.

The building blocks for successful networking are self-confidence, passion, doing your homework and being in control.

You are on stage wherever you go. You must be excited about the journey you are on to get where you want to go, and above all else, please remember to always keep a positive attitude. This can be very hard and must be practiced daily.

Most people find that being laid off is a blessing in the end. They find opportunities they never dreamed would happen for them. They start their own small business or get jobs that they never would have landed if they had stayed where they were.

I hope the time you have spent with me has sharpened your axe. Now, go cut down some trees.

All my best to you!

Jay Arbetter

About the Author

Jay Arbetter is a Senior Vice-President at UBS Financial Services. He has been a financial advisor for over 32 years and specializes in growing his clients' net worth with his proven strategies in financial planning and asset management. He is also a Chartered Special Needs Advisor.

In his spare time, he volunteers by conducting ***Networking the Old Fashion Way*** workshops all over the DFW Metroplex. Jay has a passion for working with individuals who are unemployed or want to create a business doing what they love. He also volunteers his time with several nonprofits.

His hobbies include biking, hiking, boating, trout fishing and just being outdoors. He and his wife of 31 years have two grown daughters.

Recommended Reading

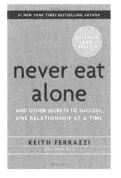

Never Eat Alone: And Other Secrets to Success, One Relationship at a Time by Keith Ferrazzi and Tahl Raz.

The bestselling business classic on the power of relationships, updated with in-depth advice for making connections in the digital world.

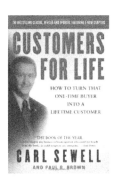

Customers for Life: How to Turn that One-time Buyer into a Lifetime Customer by Carl Sewell and Paul B. Brown.

Owner of the 2nd largest Cadillac dealership in America, Carl Sewell reveals the secret of getting customers to return again and again.

The Millionaire Next Door: The Surprising Secrets of America's Wealthy by Thomas J. Stanley and William D. Danko.

This bestselling book identifies seven common traits that show up again and again among those who have accumulated wealth.

Creating Your Excel Worksheet

You can go to www.ThePowerNetworkingStrategy.com which will take you to a Facebook page and you can download the template specifically designed to organize your Advocates.

Or, here are some quick instructions to get you started.

Worksheet - PERSONAL

- Column A – List everyone you know.
- Column B – Include their phone number.
- Column C – Add your mutual passion and interests
- Column D - How you met/how do you know them
- Column E - Note the date you will call
- Column F – Add the date you will follow up**
    o When you call them (space out calls)
    o Mentally start with why it matters, to get your mindset connection
    o Ask them a simple question i.e. do they know the name of a gardener, etc; note response. Are they willing to share / refer – else remove from your follow-up
    o Establish rapport, define needs… (sales model)
    o Notice their passion, engage conversation around MUTUAL interest (no posing)
- After you meet, follow up with them; connect with details. A phone call or thank you note is

personalized. An email is faster and gives you a trail, but it is less personal for the recipient. Note their personal style preference!
- Follow up by sharing a credible article related to their interests.

Make a List of Target Companies

- Make a list of target companies where you want to work.
- Consider nonprofits with the same passion to volunteer with; meet people, use time wisely
- Research the culture of your target companies.
- Dropping names of your target companies may evoke sharing of contacts/referrals, because it offers a specific hook.

Create a Professional Associations Worksheet

- Consider what you want to do; what professions interest you
- Attend technical organization meetings
- HR recruiters prefer personal referrals

Connections will not bond with you because they like YOU and you're fun – they will only bond with you if they think you like THEM. They should feel important. "I really admire the work you do! If everyone in my network was like you, I would be thrilled!" Remind them you respect, appreciate and value them (even if they are not people who share/refer – it is not about you).

Control the follow-up process. Get their business card (you may choose not to share / have one – so you control the follow up). Avoid handing out copies of your resume; email it after you call and follow up.

At job fairs, you hand out resumes and get the company/recruiter contact info.

Sometimes to move up, you must move out. Practice Networking!

PAGE FOR NOTES

Testimonials

"Jay, I have to write to say a big thank you for sharing so much of your life and the lessons you have learned. Your topic was networking, but I got so much more from your presentation. I cannot wait to read your book!"
Sue F.

"Your presentation has been very helpful. I am currently employed, and I'm looking. Therefore, I do not have as much time to look. I am doing what I can. It is people like you that help keep job seekers inspired. Thank you!"
JJ G.

"I was so grateful to learn networking essentials from you. I have started to make the Excel list of people I know and like. 'I love networking!' continues in my mind. It has made me more relaxed and excited about it. I have already made two appointments to meet up with two contacts this week! I am going forward so that I can pass on this information to others by living it. :) Many thanks!
Veronica K.

"Jay, enjoyed your talk on networking last night at JFS. You shared quite a few good ideas. Please include me on the email list for any future talks!"
Drake R.

"I really appreciate the networking presentation, and I've

started building the Excel worksheet! Thanks!"

Danette T.

"It was my pleasure and a great privilege learning from you. You helped me look at networking differently."

Josephine M.

"Thank you so much for taking the time to speak with the career group today at Christ United Methodist Church. It was so much more than just a networking talk! I found it to be very motivational. I'm sure you could book your speaking engagements full-time with your talent and passion!"

Andrea R.

"I enjoyed your stories and appreciated all of your great advice. Today, I'm rereading all of my notes from that night. Thank you for caring and sharing with others. May you be Blessed as much as you are a blessing to others."

Jeannie F.

"Thanks for a great presentation last Tuesday. It was sharp, to-the-point and just what I needed to hear."

LeeAnn K.

"You did a great presentation tonight. Especially enjoyed your attitude, passion and hobbies noted. You shared some great FBI and other personal stories to get the message enforced. I'm rating your talk a "10+" (scale 1 to 10) and will recommend you to other networking locations."

Stan S.

Made in the USA
Middletown, DE
28 February 2020

85338593R00089